THE COMMON HEART

THE COMMON HEART

An Experience of Interreligious Dialogue

ONE OF THE WORLD'S LONGEST-RUNNING INTERRELIGIOUS
CONFERENCES REFLECTS ON TWENTY YEARS OF DIALOGUE

The Snowmass Interreligious Conference

NETANEL MILES-YEPEZ, EDITOR

2006
Lantern Books
One Union Square West, Suite 201
New York, NY 10003

Copyright © 2006 by Netanel Miles-Yepez
1-59056-099-X

Printed in Canada

Library of Congress Cataloging-in-Publication Data

Snowmass Interreligious Conference (18th : 2004)
The common heart : an experience of interreligious dialogue : one of the world's longest-running interreligious conferences reflects on twenty years of dialogue : The Snowmass Interreligious Conference / Netanel Miles-Yepez, editor.
p. cm.
Includes bibliographical references.
ISBN 1-59056-099-X (alk. paper)
1. Religions—Congresses. I. Miles-Yepez, Nataniel M. II. Title.
BL21.S62 2004
201'.5—dc22
2006009736

To our beloved friends who have joined the celestial dialogue . . . Grandfather Gerald Red Elk, Rabbi Dovid Din, Srimata Gayatri Devi, Gesshin Prabhasa Dharma Roshi, Dr. Douglas V. Steere, and Father George Timko.

And to our generous funders, the Fetzer Institute, Ford and Susan Schumann, Walter Drake, Jr., and Mary Purcell.

CONTENTS

ACKNOWLEDGMENTS

This book is the product of a number of conversations that were the result of a twenty-year dialogue. What is presented as a "roundtable conference" in the following chapters was actually a series of separate interviews from the summer of 2004 with each of the participants of the eighteenth Snowmass Conference. At the conclusion of that conference, Edward Bastian suggested that the members collect the wisdom they had gained in twenty years of dialogue into a book, and recommended that this editor put it together for them. Mary Purcell, a member of Srimata Sudha Puri's community in La Crescenta, California, conference sponsor and observer, then generously donated the funds to create a book. We wish to thank both Ed and Mary for their insight and commitment to furthering this work.

I also wish to thank Father Thomas Keating, Tania Leontov, Roger La Borde, Swami Atmarupananda, Srimata Sudha Puri, Reverend Robert Dunbar, Dr. Edward W. Bastian, Reverend Donald Postema, Rabbi Henoch Dov Hoffman, and Dr. Ibrahim Gamard for their wonderful insights and giving attitudes throughout the interviews, and to Jim Barnett, Pema Chödrön, Roshi Bernie Glassman, Father Thomas Hopko, Imam Bilal Hyde, and Rabbi Rami Shapiro. Special thanks go to Ken Wilber, Tania Leontov and Srimata Sudha Puri: Sudha Ma's consummate note-taking and collecting of conference correspondence over the years proved invaluable to the completion of this project. Tania was not only an interviewee but also the project's able shepherdess, reading the manuscript drafts, making suggestions and corrections, and keeping the Snowmass members apprised of the book's progress. She was patient and kind through the entire process. Ken Wilber generously agreed to write the foreword and brought the insight of his unique mapmaking intellect to our humble book. All of my new friends have my thanks and appreciation. And finally, to my wife, Jennifer, and my dog, Murphy . . . thanks for the patience.

Netanel Miles-Yepez
Boulder, Colorado
November 1, 2004 (All Saints Day)

Heartfelt thanks to the generous and hospitable spiritual centers, their directors, and their communities, who hosted the Snowmass Conference. Particular thanks go to Father Joseph Boyle, whose kindness created a wonderful environment at St. Benedict's Monastery in Snowmass, Colorado, where we held, and continue to hold, many of our retreats. Also, our gratitude goes to the Fetzer Institute, Ford and Susan Schumann, Walter Drake, Jr., and Mary Purcell, our donors who funded twenty years of retreat; without their contributions and appreciation for our work, this dialogue could not have happened and there would be nothing on these pages.

Tania Leontov
Boulder, Colorado
November 1, 2004 (All Saints Day)

FOREWORD

In 1984, Father Thomas Keating invited a broad range of spiritual teachers from virtually all of the world's great wisdom traditions— Christian, Jewish, Buddhist, Hindu, indigenous, Islamic—to gather at St. Benedict's Monastery in Snowmass, Colorado. They kept no records, published no reports, filmed none of the proceedings. In fact, the results of that extraordinary gathering have been largely secret, until now.

The Common Heart is the first report of that meeting and several subsequent meetings of the same group. It is, in almost every respect, a rather amazing document—first in that the meetings could and did happen, and second in the results, at once startling and reassuring.

A student once asked me, "Why study the tangled web of the world's traditional religions?" The implication was that the many of these religions were old, outdated, and more or less worthless; and further, they all disagreed with one another anyway, so why bother?

I replied that, yes, they were "old," and yes, they mostly disagreed with one another. "But every now and then," I said, "you find profound points of agreement among all of them. And any time you find something that all of the world's religions agree on, you may want to pay very, very close attention, yes?"

This document is an example of some of those agreements and therefore, I believe, something we may want to pay very, very close attention to.

I realize that academic attempts to show certain common threads in the world's great religions—from Aldous Huxley's *Perennial Philosophy* to Huston Smith's *Forgotten Truth*—have all been attacked by postmodernists as essentially meaningless, because even though writers such as Huxley and Smith purported to show cross-religion similarities, cultural relativism asserts that these similarities cannot be real. Actual cultures and traditions, the charge goes, are all islands unto themselves, with massive incommensurability blocking passage or even communication between them. There can be no universal spirit because nothing universal can be known or, therefore, said to exist in any meaningful sense. So there can be no agreement between, say, Taoist texts and Christian texts about Ultimate Reality.

But Father Thomas Keating did not assemble texts in a room; he assembled human beings who, quite apart from any help from the postmodern poststructuralists, were able to decide whether their respective spiritual traditions agreed on certain points. And in fact, these human beings from very different backgrounds and traditions—cultural, linguistic, social, individual—did arrive at several profound points of agreement about what, by any other name, is Ultimate Reality. The wonderful, intense, difficult, playful, and respectful interreligious dialogues by which the participants arrived at these conclusions—of both important similarities and wonderful differences—are the core of this extraordinary book.

And so it turns out that, even across different cultures and religions, meaningful human communication and agreement can and does occur, especially when the heart is silent and listens with respect. (And I have noticed, anyway, that postmodernists from different cultures seem to understand one another just fine—a bit of an embarrassment for the whole theory, what?)

As for these points of agreement, what are we to make of them? The first one is: "The world's religions bear witness to the experience of Ultimate Reality, to which they give various names." I ask, because in today's world there looms a very difficult issue that simply must be addressed: Why is it that, at first glance, the world's religions—or the ones the public hears about on the news—seem to be the major source of human conflict, when, on the other hand, dialogues like these show that spirituality could be the primary source of peace among humankind? This paradox is so large, so jarring, and so hard to reconcile. It is made all the worse when beheadings in the name of God occur weekly, bombings in the name of God occur daily, and no world religion has a history totally free of such. I believe that unless we can find a way to understand and differentiate those two extremes of religion, both will be deeply suspect in today's world.

Let me suggest one way to think about this, and let me give a frightfully abbreviated version (please see *The Eye of Spirit* for a more detailed look). Studies in developmental psychology over the last few decades show that individuals tend to undergo an unmistakable trajectory of human growth and development, from preconventional stages to conventional stages to postconventional, or from prerational to rational to transrational, or from egocentric to ethnocentric to worldcentric. Without pigeonholing anybody or any tradition—because people and traditions can span the entire spectrum—there is a world of difference between those who are acting in egocentric, preconventional, and prerational ways, and those acting in postconventional, worldcentric, and transrational ways. The latter, having developed and befriended rationality, now transcend and include it; whereas the former are not acting beyond reason, but beneath it.

It is the bane of contemplative dialogues such as these that, in the common mind, preconventional and postconventional are lumped together, and prerational and transrational are unceremoniously equated, when they are quite literally poles apart. But for today's conventional, rationally minded individual, the world's great contemplative and transrational mystics and realizers are indistinguishable from irrational fanatics or those seized with infantile oceanic fantasies.

This is not only sad, it is a cultural catastrophe of the first magnitude. And yet, until religion itself learns how to convey these differences convincingly and increasingly focus on the best in its postconventional, transpersonal, and contemplative dimensions, religion for the world at large will likely remain the province of either prerational fanatics or rational cynics. Transrational dialogues such as these—which embrace rationality fully and then go beyond it into the mystery of the divine and the obviousness of the ultimate—will never gain the deep appreciation and even reverence they deserve.

The points of agreement in the following dialogues do indeed spring from that deep space of transrational openness and contemplative transparency, where the human heart stands naked before the divine, discovering at the end of that journey into the present a dividing line between them that is almost impossible to find, a gateless gate to that I AM–ness that only alone is.

And what are the rest of these extraordinary points of agreement, these things with which the world's religions can concur? Please start reading and sharing in these dialogues from the Unborn and Undying, and know that you are indeed on a journey into your very own heart, a common ground that is timeless and therefore eternally present, spaceless and therefore infinitely open, an Ultimate Reality that is reading this page, holding this book in its hands, and looking out through your very own eyes in this very present moment, for where else could the journey possibly begin and end?

Ken Wilber
Denver, Colorado
Winter 2005

NOTE TO THE READER

Gendered language is still a problem in our world, and the difficulty remains around using masculine or feminine personal pronouns with regard to God and entities of nonspecific gender. Please be aware that such occurrences of masculine language in this book do not reflect the attitude of patriarchal dominance, but are simply vestiges of a paradigm we have left behind before evolving a gender-neutral personal pronoun.

Also, some may object to the use of the words *ecumenism* and *ecumenical*, because these are words that have traditionally described cooperative situations between differing parts of the Christian Church, or other inter-Christian dialogues. However, the Greek original, *oikoumenikos*, simply means "from the whole world." It is in this inclusive sense that we use the word *ecumenical*. At the same time, we also honor the word's longtime association with dialogue and cooperation.

N. M-Y.

"THE POINTS OF AGREEMENT"

FATHER THOMAS KEATING, OCSO

In 1984, I invited a group of spiritual teachers from a variety of the world religions—Buddhist, Hindu, Jewish, Islamic, Native American, Russian Orthodox, Protestant, and Roman Catholic—to gather at St. Benedict's Monastery in Snowmass, Colorado, to meditate together in silence, and to share our personal spiritual journeys, especially those elements in our respective traditions that have proved most helpful to us along the way.

We kept no record and published no papers. As our trust and friendship grew, we felt moved to investigate various points that we seemed to agree on. The original points of agreement were worked over during the course of subsequent meetings as we continued to meet for a week or so each year, leaving us with the following points:

1. The world religions bear witness to the experience of Ultimate Reality, to which they give various names.
2. Ultimate Reality cannot be limited by any name or concept.
3. Ultimate Reality is the ground of infinite potentiality and actualization.
4. Faith is opening, accepting, and responding to Ultimate Reality. Faith in this sense precedes every belief system.
5. The potential for human wholeness—or, in other frames of reference, enlightenment, salvation, transcendence, transformation, blessedness—is present in every human being.
6. Ultimate Reality may be experienced not only through religious practices, but also through nature, art, human relationships, and service to others.
7. As long as the human condition is experienced as separate from Ultimate Reality, it is subject to ignorance and illusion, weakness and suffering.

8. Disciplined practice is essential to the spiritual life; yet spiritual attainment is not the result of one's own efforts, but the result of the experience of oneness with Ultimate Reality.

During our third conference at Karmê Chöling in Vermont, in May of 1986, we came up with additional points of agreement of a practical nature:

1. Some examples of disciplined practice, common to us all:
    a. Practice of compassion
    b. Service to others
    c. Practicing moral precepts and virtues
    d. Training in meditation techniques and regularity of practice
    e. Attention to diet and exercise
    f. Fasting and abstinence
    g. The use of music, chanting, and sacred symbols
    h   Practice in awareness (recollection, mindfulness) and living in the present moment
    i. Pilgrimage
    j. Study of scriptural texts and scriptures

    And in some traditions:
    k. Relationship with a qualified teacher
    l. Repetition of sacred words
    m. Observing periods of silence and solitude
    n. Movement and dance
    o. Formative community

2. It is essential to extend our formal practice of awareness into all the aspects of our life.
3. Humility, gratitude, and a sense of humor are indispensable in the spiritual life.
4. Prayer is communion with Ultimate Reality, whether it is regarded as personal, impersonal, or beyond them both.

We were surprised and delighted to find so many points of similarity and convergence in our respective paths. Like most people of our time, we originally expected that we would find practically nothing in common. In the years that followed, we spontaneously and somewhat hesitatingly began to take a closer look at certain points of disagreement until these became our main focus of attention. We found that discussing our points of disagreement increased the bonding of the group even more than discovering our points of agreement. We became more honest in stating frankly what we believed and why, without at the same time making any effort to convince others of our own position. We simply presented our understanding as a gift to the group.

Today, we would like to present these "Points of Agreement" as a gift to all who will welcome them, to all who will use them to promote understanding.

If you are going to give a gift, give what is most precious to you, because anything less is just throwing away your trash to someone else. . . . If they are one of the 'people,' don't be upset if they don't have it the next time you see them.

—Grandfather Gerald Red Elk, 1984

THE SNOWMASS ROUNDTABLE

In the Summer of 2004, the members of the Snowmass Interreligious Conference (hereafter, simply the Snowmass Conference) who participated in Snowmass XVIII at St. Benedict's Monastery, Snowmass, Colorado, celebrating twenty years of dialogue together, were interviewed by Netanel Miles-Yepez, in an attempt to capture the uniqueness and wisdom of one of the world's longest-running interreligious dialogue groups. The participants in this dialogue included:

- Netanel Miles-Yepez (Moderator of the Snowmass Roundtable, 2004)
- Swami Atmarupananda (Member of the Snowmass Conference, 1995–2004)
- Dr. Edward W. Bastian (Member of the Snowmass Conference, 1999–2004)
- Reverend Robert B. Dunbar (Member of the Snowmass Conference, 1987–2004)
- Dr. Ibrahim Gamard (Member of the Snowmass Conference, 1988–2004)
- Rabbi Henoch Dov Hoffman (Member of the Snowmass Conference, 1995–2004)
- Father Thomas Keating (Convener/Member of the Snowmass Conference, 1984–2004)
- Roger La Borde (Member of the Snowmass Conference, 1985–2004)
- Tania Leontov (Member of the Snowmass Conference, 1984–2004)
- Reverend Donald H. Postema (Member of the Snowmass Conference, 1988–2004)
- Srimata Sudha Puri (Member of the Snowmass Conference, 1985–2004)

Looking back on the Snowmass dialogues, I think there are two questions that, when answered, will tell us why it was a success: What was the original intention of the dialogue? And what was the intention of the participants?
—Jim Barnett, 2004

CHAPTER ONE

ORIGINS AND IDEALS

A NEW KIND OF DIALOGUE

Netanel Miles-Yepez: *Father Keating, what was your purpose in founding the Snowmass Conference?*

Thomas Keating: I always saw myself as more of a "convener" than a "founder." It was really just a big experiment in the beginning, and I didn't know how it would all work out.

I began planning it in 1983 after taking part in a series of Christian–Buddhist dialogues at the Naropa Institute in Boulder, Colorado. During these "dialogues," I noticed that we, the dialoguers, weren't speaking to one another so much as we were addressing the audience. But, on the two occasions when the conveners succeeded in bringing us together a day before the conference, we got on very well and actually got to talk to one another as peers, albeit all too briefly. So I asked myself, what would happen if the whole point was just to get together and talk, without an audience? And what if it was broader than just a Buddhist–Christian dialogue? So, that was the initial motive for getting that first group of teachers together at St. Benedict's Monastery in Snowmass, Colorado, where this began, and where it got its name, the "Snowmass Conference" (though we didn't always meet there).

Netanel Miles-Yepez: *So, the primary purpose was to take the dialogue out of the public arena because you had noticed that the audience was influencing and impeding the intimacy of the dialogue?*

Thomas Keating: It seemed to me that it was *dominating* the dialogue. The rich interchanges glimpsed in those brief periods we spent together before the conferences began, were all but non-existent when we came before an audience. So, I thought, let's just come together to talk about what helps us most in our spiritual practice. This, it seemed, would be far more fruitful, and, hopefully, we would come to a better understanding of the terms we were using to communicate. You know, you can use the same term, but if you are interpreting it in your own way, from your own cultural background, and the person you are dialoguing with is presupposing his or her own interpretation is meant, then there is a lot of confusion.

Netanel Miles-Yepez: *But, over the years, the Snowmass Conference did do the occasional public dialogue, didn't it?*

Thomas Keating: Yes, there were three or four occasions when we had brief meetings with the people in the neighborhood who wanted to come, but we didn't do too well in that environment.

Netanel Miles-Yepez: *Was it a public failure or a private disappointment? Sudha?*

Sudha Puri: It was a "private disappointment." Often they were actually quite successful from the standpoint of the audience. One of the more successful was at the Harmonium Mundi Conference in California, the year His Holiness the Dalai Lama got the Nobel Peace Prize. Mataji and Father Thomas spoke, and it was really one of the hits of the conference, because a number of the attendees had heard about the Snowmass Conference— that we had bonded in an amazing way—and were eager to hear more about it. And the truth was, we were eager to bring some of the richness of what we were experiencing to others . . . but, generally, the dialogue ended up feeling artificial for us. We weren't sharing at the same level, not really; we were performing in a sense. So, even though these occasions were great successes from the perspective of the audience, none of us felt satisfied by the experience, because the essence of the Snowmass Conference was built on camaraderie and real honesty.

Netanel Miles-Yepez: *I'm curious, Father Keating; what criteria did you use in bringing such a group together?*

Thomas Keating: Really, it was all word of mouth. I had heard good things about one or another of these people, and I just extended them invitations. I wanted to do more than just a Buddhist–Christian dialogue, so I invited as broad a spectrum of people as I could.

Netanel Miles-Yepez: *Tania, Sudha and Roger—you were all at that first meeting in 1984; would you mind telling how you came to be there?*

Tania Leontov: At that time I was living in Boulder, Colorado, near my teacher, Chögyam Trungpa Rinpoche. And while Father Keating was participating in the Buddhist–Christian dialogues with Rinpoche and others at the Naropa Institute, I was hosting him in my home, and we had some very inspiring conversations of our own.

I remember him telling me at that time how inspired he was by the dialogues he had done, but also how he regretted that some of the participants felt pressure to represent, or to be "standard-bearers" for their tradition's dogma and view when the dialogue was held as a public event. So, he was proposing to hold a private retreat for a group of interfaith leaders where they would get a chance to talk without having to support a "public face." He felt that this kind of intimate personal dialogue might be more productive in terms of true interfaith cooperation and appreciation. He also hoped that changes might come from this kind of deep sharing, bringing a measure of peace and sanity to the world.

When I heard this, I was possessed by a total passion to be a part of that conference! I couldn't say why, but I simply had to be part of it. However, my real question was, how? I really didn't feel particularly qualified; I was a teacher of Buddhism and Buddhist meditation, but I was not remotely a spiritual leader in the sense Father Tom was. So, after wrestling with my doubts, I finally called him and said, "I realize I am putting you on the spot . . . *and trading on our friendship* . . . but I really want to be part of this conference. And I will understand completely if you say no. But he didn't.

Netanel Miles-Yepez: *Do you know why you had to be a part of it now?*

Tania Leontov: Interfaith work is almost all that I am doing now in terms of both my livelihood and passion. I didn't know where the inspiration came from, but it continues to shape my life in a profound way. There is wisdom held in our spiritual paths that the world needs badly, a contact with something vast in our narrow lives, a small opening that might help to change the terrible things that are going on in our world.

Roger La Borde: It's interesting, shortly before he died, Grandfather Gerald Red Elk told me how closely he held this group to his heart . . . he believed it was a good sign that sanity still existed in the world.

I came into the group because of Gerald. Father Keating had contacted me after hearing about the now-famous meeting between Trungpa Rinpoche and Gerald at Red Feather Lakes, Colorado. Gerald was my adopted uncle and I had helped to arrange that meeting, so Tom was obviously given my name by someone in Trungpa's *sangha* ["community"]. When he called, he gave me a thumbnail sketch of what he intended to do with this group, and asked if I would convey an invitation to Gerald. So, I called Gerald on the reservation in Montana, gave him the background, and he said, "I will go, but only if you come with me." I told Gerald, "They aren't inviting me, they're inviting you." But he only said, "Well, you have to be there, you have things to say, you have things to do. So, you tell them I am not coming unless you go. Tell them you are my assistant."

So, when I called Tom back, as you can imagine from what we have already said, he was not too happy about the idea of having an "observer," but acquiesced to Gerald's request. As it turned out, I already knew Pema [Chödrön], who was in the group that year, so Gerald and I shared a ride with her, Tania and Yuen Yi from Boulder to Snowmass.

Sudha Puri: As with Roger, the group sort of inherited me. When Father Thomas invited Mataji to be a representative of Hinduism and Vedanta to the group, I was chosen to be her companion. She was getting older, and it was a necessity for her to have someone nearby. And I was thrilled to come, even as an observer.

Netanel Miles-Yepez: *Both you and Roger were invited to become members during the second Snowmass Conference in 1985; how did that come about?*

Sudha Puri: In 1985, Mataji named me as her successor, and I suppose that brought me up in the world a bit. But, likely it was more practical than that. We had decided not to record the meetings at the first conference, and since I was really an ace note taker, I could pretty much get the talk verbatim. So I was able to become indispensable to the group. Since the second conference was held at our ashram in La Crescenta, California, I was the travel agent for the group, and got to know everyone a little better.

Roger La Borde: As an observer the first year, during mealtimes and breaks, I had a number of wonderful conversations and walks with various members, but I had formed a special connection with Rabbi Rami Shapiro.

The first meeting was pretty much taken up with whether the conference would be recorded or if they were just going to allow notes to be taken. Then, after that was settled, the discussion turned to finding "points of common agreement." So, after a couple of days, they arrived at a "point" which said, "Daily disciplined meditation is essential for spiritual awakening." I had been biting my tongue for two days, but now I finally felt I had to speak up. I said, "May I ask a question?" And Rami immediately answered, "Yes." But then someone else said, "Are we going to allow an observer to participate?" I understand now how this must have seemed like the group was degenerating into the "public" situation Tom was describing before. Nevertheless, Rami piped in again and said, "He's not an observer; we want to hear what he has to say."

Rami was a big supporter and protector of mine in the first couple of years, and in the second year he jumped in at the beginning and said, "Roger is a part of this group, not an observer," and by that time, everyone else seemed to agree.

THE RIGHT ENVIRONMENT

Netanel Miles-Yepez: *I want to return for a moment to the idea of a "retreat" for spiritual teachers; given that this was the intention, was having the dialogue in the right environment a consideration?*

Ibrahim Gamard: I really believe a spiritual setting is critical to the success of the meetings. It just worked better when it was held in a spiritual center of some kind, in a place where there was a spiritual community for support. One time, we met at Nada Hermitage in Crestone, Colorado. There was such a spiritual atmosphere there; I remember well the presence I felt in its little chapel and the aura of spiritual energy there. But my first session, on the other hand, which was one of the rare occasions when we met in a secular environment, felt *less* spiritual . . . except when our group meditated together. The setting just wasn't a place of prayer and meditation.

Donald Postema: Most of our meeting places gave me a sense of being on retreat. We made space in the schedule for private time: hiking, rest, reading and enjoying nature. I've always come two days early and stayed a few days after the meeting for private retreat.

Tania Leontov: For a very realized person, I suppose environment is irrelevant. But, for the rest of us, environment can really invite positive, or receptive, states of mind and feeling. And we felt the difference. When the conference was happening at a spiritual center, it was always very inviting, whether it was a Christian monastery, a Hindu ashram, or a Buddhist *gompa*. There was something in the fact that the things we were talking about were important in these environments, and they in turn *expressed* what we were talking about. Spiritual communities, intentional architecture, and physical beauty really communicate a support to the dialogue.

In Trungpa Rinpoche's tradition, there is no question that environment is part of the teaching. It is called "sign lineage"— the phenomenal world signals and speaks—so you create an environment that speaks of an invitation to certain states of mind. When you are finding your way, as we were, it makes a lot of difference. The one occasion when we went to a hotel, it was horrible, and part of it was the environment. Having the right environment is really crucial.

Roger La Borde: One of the problems with the hotel was the separation. Being housed together, having easy access to one another, and sharing the whole experience are very important. If we were too spread out and had to commute to come to a central facility for a meeting, that was also a problem.

Sudha Puri: The one really negative experience I remember, in terms of environment, was when we were hosted by a religion department on a college campus. Sadly, a member of the department had died just before we arrived, and the poor dean who was supposed to be our host could spare us practically no time at all. Even worse, the meeting room for our sessions was actually the anteroom of her office, which, because of the death in the department, was filled with a constant stream of the bereaved coming and going.

The instability of the whole situation seemed to seep into our group dynamic. Two guest members were having difficulty getting along, and Gessin Prabhasa Dharma Roshi was constantly acting as an intermediary to bring them together. It was her first meeting, and it is a wonder that she ever came back. It was strange situation with a lot of drama, and we weren't able to get off the ground very well. The two real bright spots of that meeting were the introductions of Gesshin and Rabbi Dovid Din to the group.

Atmarupananda: Most of the meetings I have been to have taken place at Snowmass, so I would even want to say that consistency of place helps; it's like going to the same place to meditate each day; when you get into that space, you are ready for meditation because all the associations are there. Just walking onto the grounds at Snowmass year after year, I felt ready for dialogue; you don't have to spend as much time settling in.

Donald Postema: It is inspiring to come to a place where a spiritual life is already going on, as it is at a monastery or ashram; we didn't have to create a holy space, it was already there. We simply entered the spiritual atmosphere. The monks at Snowmass provided a hospitable environment that I think influenced how we viewed each other, talked with each other and related to each other.

Robert Dunbar: I feel the same way; it made every difference to meet at Snowmass. For me, it is our home base. And when we're there, I think we are at our best. It is simply a sacred setting and opens up the right channels.

PARTICIPANTS AND WISDOM HOLDERS

Netanel Miles-Yepez: *If the "spiritual quality" of the place matters this much, how does a person's spiritual quality affect the dynamic of dialogue? After all, this must be a consideration in maintaining such a group?*

Thomas Keating: I am certainly not qualified to judge anybody, but it is usually obvious that some people have been more exposed to the levels of spirituality that are considered more advanced in all the traditions, and it *can* affect the quality of the dialogue.

Sudha Puri: It is always a difficult situation when it becomes obvious that a guest member has not spent time in developing his or her own inner life. And I don't mean to imply a spiritual elitism here; it simply unbalances the dialogue to a degree. Often the person is quite knowledgeable about the surface of their tradition, but unfamiliar with its contemplative depths. In many ways, the dialogue of the Snowmass Conference relies on a common experience of contemplative depth.

On the other end is the occasional person who is not even familiar with his or her own tradition, and thus is not able to contribute to dialogue in any significant way. As Father Thomas says, "You have to be really grounded in your own tradition to be able to give and receive intelligently, to contribute and build what the particular meeting is trying to build." So that has been an occasional problem.

Netanel Miles-Yepez: *What do you do in such a situation?*

Thomas Keating: Well, it happens, and it's important to reserve judgment, remembering that everybody's contribution is nothing more than that, a contribution. And we cannot discount that growth may also occur as a result of the dialogue itself.

Netanel Miles-Yepez: *This doesn't seem to have been much of an issue in the beginning.*

Sudha Puri: No, it wasn't. Just as an observer that first year, it was quite an experience. These people were really peers, and it was not often that they had the opportunity to be with their peers on a spiritual level. Father Thomas chose a pretty amazing group of people: Mataji, my beloved teacher; Grandfather Gerald Red Elk, a loveable Lakota Sioux medicine man who was so willing to share and who had such amazing insights; and Dr. Douglas Steere, a beautiful Quaker who worked behind the scenes for world peace, doing difficult negotiations in areas of conflict around the world. These were great souls and real saints. I would also include Father Thomas and Gesshin Prabhasa Dharma Roshi in that category. I listened intently to every word that came out of Father Thomas's mouth; I really consider him a modern prophet.

It didn't take long for these people to establish a real trust and intimacy—to be able to share and reveal things candidly. Deeply spiritual people often have wonderful senses of humor and a real spontaneity. And we were privileged to see a lot of it.

Roger La Borde: Gerald and I used to laugh till our sides ached! He was an amazing human being. In his youth, he had been a very angry alcoholic, and by the 1960s he was in the hospital dying from it. As he put it, he was "dying of anger, hate, chain-smoking, and drinking." Then he prayed for a second chance, and promised to stop smoking, drinking, hating, and to go back to the old ways to help his people.

I'll tell you, I don't think I ever heard Gerald say anything worse than, "That person has a negative attitude." In the end, his people included everyone, not just red men, but everyone he met. He was definitely a universal being.

Tania Leontov: To be around genuine wisdom holders is a very different experience. In many ways, they are very ordinary, but their view and presence emanate something special. It makes a difference in the environment. At this point, we have lost most of our elder wisdom holders, and only Father Keating is left to us.

It's hard to say just what their special quality is; they are more accommodating than ordinary people, but can also have a very sharp clarity that cuts through the nonsense. I am thinking of Gayatri Devi's razor sharp mind, and Father Keating's rapier-like thrusts at dogmatists. So it's not just kindness; their compassion is palpable. They also have a way of finding the unifying principles and helping to expose them. And when they speak there is a sense of enormous courage. If you are on a path with them, just being in the presence of these qualities invites your own best qualities to emerge. It makes you understand what humans are capable of, and of what you are capable. When you quail and hide out and see someone genuinely and with great simplicity being very brave, you can feel it, and it helps to create a map for you of where you need to go. Those of us who have come across spiritual masters carry that map with us, the sound of that voice in our ears, and the feeling of their compassion in our hearts. It makes a tremendous difference.

There was at least one year when Father Tom couldn't attend, and I felt that the light almost went out of the group. There was a sense that we were more likely to end up in "smaller mind" without him.

Netanel Miles-Yepez: *Father Keating, you have been much discussed here, perhaps you would like to weigh in with some of your own feelings about dialogue with "wisdom holders?"*

Thomas Keating: Well, I'll exclude myself from that category, but I suppose, at this point, I can't avoid the role of "elder." However, twenty years ago there were wonderful members whom I could still look to as elders, and I admired them greatly. A significant person in that first group was Gayatri Devi, from whom I learned a great deal about the Hindu tradition, especially the *bhakti* tradition, of which she was a marvelous embodiment. We became very close friends.

But, some of my most significant dialogues with "wisdom holders" happened when I was still abbot of St. Joseph's Abbey in Spencer, Massachusetts. At the time, a number of teachers were coming to the West. Just a half-hour up the road from the monastery was an Insight Meditation center that drew a number of outstanding *vipassana* teachers from the Buddhist Theravada tradition, and they often came down and visited us. One of these was Ajahn Cha. I was very impressed with him, and we had a great time together; he had the same kinds of problems in his monastery as I was having in mine, and we had great fun comparing notes! He was like an old shoe. He reminded me a lot of Pope John the XXIII, whom I had met briefly, and whom I also admired greatly. He was really laid back. He had a very strict monastery, and I don't know what he was like there, but he was friendliness itself when he visited us. So he was one important "wisdom holder."

Another was Joshu Sasaki Roshi of Mount Baldy in Los Angeles. Just before we met, he was actually about to head for Europe to look for Trappist monasteries there, since he had heard ours were most similar to the Zen Buddhist monasteries of Japan. So when he heard about St. Joseph's Abbey, he decided that he didn't have to go quite so far. Anyway, he came and offered to give us a *sesshin* (a period of intense meditation training), and we accepted. And after that, he came to the monastery about twice a year for about ten years offering sesshin. Fortunately, I was able to get to most of them and hear his teachings first hand.

Sasaki Roshi's broad-mindedness was an inspiration to me, because he was looking to teach Christians Zen. For him, Zen was not the property of Japan, or even Buddhism, but a kind of universal religious attitude. I admired that perspective and have adopted it in my own life. I found the little exposure I had to Zen extremely helpful, and Sasaki Roshi's *taishos* very mind expanding. At one time, someone suggested that he come to the Snowmass Conference, but the fact that he needed a translator got in the way.

Gesshin Prabhasa Dharma Roshi was a student of Sasaki Roshi for a long time. Actually, she had already had an enlightening experience before she started with Sasaki Roshi, but she needed an articulation of that experience from him. By the time I met her, she was one of the most articulate Zen Buddhists in the West.

Netanel Miles-Yepez: *Was there a conscious effort over the years to try and invite people of this quality?*

Sudha Puri: We relied on referrals for the most part, but we were always hopeful, and got lucky most of the time. I think, however, we did avoid people who we felt were too "high-profile" for our group. We tried to find people who were leaders, without necessarily being international figures. We wanted to operate under the radar in a certain respect, and just talk issues. Nevertheless, many of our members, like Pema [Chödrön] and Father Keating, became international figures as the years passed, and I think it has served to put out "the good news" about our dialogue.

Donald Postema: I'm one of those who came to the Snowmass Conference by word of mouth. In 1988, I went on a sabbatical spiritual journey for seven months, visiting monasteries, retreat houses, Buddhist centers, and Hindu ashrams in the western part of the United States. But, before I left, a woman in Ann Arbor told me about Anada Ashram in California, and also sent them a copy of my book, *Space for God*. So I ended up visiting the ashram, and really got to know and appreciate Gayatri Devi and Sudha. Later I realized that they were probably checking me out too, to see whether a Calvinist could be spiritual or contemplative enough to be a member of the Snowmass Conference. Toward the end of my stay, they invited me to the Snowmass gathering at Mount Holyoke that spring.

Edward Bastian: It is definitely a balancing act finding the right people. You ask the opinions of people you trust, people who are of the same quality you are looking for and then you test the chemistry. Are they sincere, kind and engaging? Do they share the deep desire to dialogue? Do they have a contemplative practice and a deep knowledge of their tradition? These are all important questions, and important ingredients. But I also agree with Father Keating: once someone is in the dialogue space with you, you have to let go of the judgments, and even if it seems that they are lacking in some of these qualities, you have to be aware of the great power a dialogue like this can have on an individual and their spiritual development. And I think most of us can attest to this for ourselves.

Netanel Miles-Yepez: *Ed, you are the newest member of the group; what was it like to enter a group of old friends?*

Edward Bastian: It felt great. I was really honored, and it was a special experience to be among them. I had heard so much about the

Snowmass Conference; it had a reputation for doing deep contemplative work between teachers and leaders of different traditions. So I was excited.

I was invited by Father Keating as a representative of
Buddhism that year because Tania could not make it, and like her
I didn't feel particularly qualified. But after a few deep discussions
with Father Keating about my interest in developing an interfaith
foundation, he convinced me that it would be useful for me to
attend and see how it worked in the Snowmass Conference.

Netanel Miles-Yepez: *Did you feel welcomed by the group?*

Edward Bastian: Without a doubt, I was welcomed with open arms,
and after our first couple of meditations and dialogues together I
already felt I had two new friends in Father George Timko and
Swami Atmarupananda.

INTIMACY AND THE "PUBLIC FACE"

Netanel Miles-Yepez: *Earlier, both Sudha Ma and Roger mentioned
the issue of whether or not the meetings would be recorded; how
was this decided?*

Thomas Keating: When the question was raised, "Do we want to tape
some of this?" Grandfather Gerald Red Elk said, "No, that would
not be good, because then we would be hesitant about people back
home hearing what we say. This is intimate stuff, and I think we
should not share it outside the group. If the wisdom needs to be
heard, it will be heard." That won the favor of everyone, and we've
never taped a conference, but we did ask Sudha to take notes.

Sudha Puri: I remember when Grandfather Red Elk said this, an
eagle flew by the window, and this was taken as a sign.

Roger La Borde: When Gerald had his dialogue with Trungpa
Rinpoche, there was a tape recorder sitting on a wrought-iron

table next to them, and someone asked permission to tape them. Gerald's response was, "If it is meant to tape, it will; if it is not, it won't." It didn't.

Netanel Miles-Yepez: *Grandfather Red Elk's comments bring us back to Father Keating's initial insight, i.e., that this should be a dialogue of intimacy and not of dogmas repeated for public consumption. So, given that the meetings were not recorded, and that they were held in an intimate setting where everyone could speak openly, how did it feel to finally engage in a dialogue where it didn't matter who was listening? Did it change the dynamic for you? Swami Atmarupananda?*

Atmarupananda: It changed the dynamic in a very positive way. This was a dialogue where we didn't have to think about our "public face," but only about what was in our hearts; we could share openly with people who weren't going to go out and say things out of context, and make difficult situations for any of us. This was one of the most attractive features of the Snowmass Conference to me.

Tania Leontov: Another attractive aspect for me is the fact that I don't have pretend to be less inspired than I really am in this group, to show that I care about what I'm saying. This just isn't encouraged and supported in some environments.

Netanel Miles-Yepez: *But even when one doesn't have to maintain appearances, we still have our commitments, our "rootedness" in a particular path, so what remains of the "public face" that is important in the dialogue . . . or that may hinder it?*

Atmarupananda: Obviously, as Sudha was saying earlier, there would not be much use in having a Hindu or a Muslim in a dialogue group who couldn't really represent their tradition, that is to say, one who didn't have the essential knowledge of the tradition and rootedness in it—after all, losing the "public face" doesn't mean becoming an amorphous spiritual entity with no perspective and depth. The absence of the need to protect a "public face" simply allows us to speak from the standpoint of our tradition, but more personally than a flat theological stand would allow.

I have had positive and negative experiences with the "public face" in dialogue. Some people have a much harder time than others relaxing into the dialogue situation, and some are not able to overcome it. In that instance, the person is bound up in an organizational, dogmatic identity that will not allow them to speak openly.

Donald Postema: In the group, we are encouraged and expected to *represent* our respective traditions as authentically as possible. This serves a couple of purposes: first, it gives the group a more realistic picture of where you are coming from, and secondly, it lets the "representative" know that he or she needn't feel pressured to water anything down, to make it more palatable for the group.

Netanel Miles-Yepez: *I remember Raimundo Panikkar [a Catholic priest with deep connections to the Hindu tradition] saying, "I can say whatever I like as long as I make it clear that I am not speaking for the Catholic Church." So he has a certain freedom, but makes it clear what is his own personal view and what is the Church's doctrine.*

Donald Postema: Yes, we like to say that our members are speaking *from* a tradition, not *for* a tradition. We try to be authentic, but no one is expected to speak *for* their particular tradition. We aren't here giving presentations, we have to drop the roles to some degree, and just try to have a rich and honest sharing on a number of levels.

Atmarupananda: No one can toe one hundred percent of an organizational line; people are too complex for that.

Tania Leontov: I feel that I have to be true to my tradition only as *I* understand it. You know, we belong to particular traditions because they inspire us (hopefully), but our experience often leads us to have views that vary somewhat from the "party line."

CHAPTER TWO

OPENING A DIALOGUE

BREAKING THE ICE: THE FIRST SESSION

Netanel Miles-Yepez: *Father Keating, how did you go about getting to know one another and "breaking the ice" at the first Snowmass Conference?*

Thomas Keating: During the first session, we started out just sharing our spiritual journeys, who we were, where we came from, and what we were concerned about. This has been the model for our first session ever since. Except that now it is more about how things have been for us in the past year, what we are doing now, and what are our current issues—basically renewing our friendships. But that very first session, we deliberately had no purpose except to introduce ourselves. It was just a dialogue of the heart.

Netanel Miles-Yepez: *Why do you think this worked? Tania?*

Tania Leontov: On one level, it's an obvious first step: get to know one another. But on a deeper level, the reason it continues to work, I think, is this: When people are deeply involved in spiritual practice, their day-to-day lives are not separate from their spirituality; what is going on in their lives is an expression of their spiritual path. Secular Western culture tends to parse our lives up—this is our work, this is our play, this is what we love to do, this is our family time—but the spiritual path asks you to integrate all of it. In Buddhism, we say, "bring everything to the path" . . . the belly-ache, the arguments, all of that is the spiritual path.

When we first started, I think everyone was on their best behavior as representatives of their traditions. But things started to open up fairly quickly as people began to become aware of the opportunity to be had here. Many of them had not been in a situation that had invited them to talk about the integration and deep experience of their path before; this is really an intimate situation when you are a spiritual teacher, to talk about "the dark night of the soul," the problems you have with your bureaucracy, boundary issues, and your personal inspiration.

Sudha Puri: I agree, this is where the trust was built; it is where we aired our laundry and really supported one another. It was in this session, in Vermont, when we went through **Swami Buddhananda**'s decision to leave being a swami; I felt privileged to be among those he felt he could share this decision with, and the issues behind it. And then we had the pleasure of getting to know him again as Jim Barnett in Sedona!

Later, when Mataji was sick, and I was dealing with my own health problems, and there were tensions in the ashram, this is where we talked about them. Ma couldn't be what she had been for people, and some devotees were expecting her to give at the same level, and suddenly they weren't there for *her* anymore. In many ways, she was even more powerful spiritually, but somehow they didn't feel it. That was a very difficult period in my life, and it was safe to talk about it among my peers and friends at Snowmass. It was a totally supportive environment. It was understood, what happens in the group stays in the group.

Tania Leontov: I just want to add that this kind of support and catching up always went well beyond the first session; we were catching up from the moment we arrived, and continued these informal dialogues at every opportunity.

Netanel Miles-Yepez: *Tania brings up an interesting point, and Roger alluded to this earlier: the time spent informally together, taking meals and walks together between the formal dialogues, is often just as fruitful as the structured aspect, and perhaps more so. It has* *been my experience that the informal dialogues inform and enrich the formal dialogue. Did anyone else find this to be the case?*

Thomas Keating: Yes, often more came from the casual, informal dialogues we had than the formal. This is even starting to happen in some public dialogue situations. For instance, Ed Bastian tries to make sure that his speakers share living arrangements and meals, and have plenty of time to "break the ice" before going on the platform at his Spiritual Paths seminars.

Ibrahim Gamard: I think people are just more likely to be self-disclosing in these intimate personal encounters. Many times, after an intense session, there would be a lot to process, and various combinations of people would come together to talk further about the formal dialogue. And, of course, this continued at the dinner table, and I found these discussions both rich and rewarding.

Atmarupananda: Like Father Keating, I have also been a participant in Ed's Spiritual Paths seminars, which seem to me to be somewhat of an extension of our work in the Snowmass Conference. There, we have found that getting the presenters together—often a day ahead of the presentations—was important for getting to know each other. When you are coming in cold to a situation, even if you are used to dialogue, and if you don't know where the others are coming from, it makes it much harder. You can still make a speech, but working with them is much harder. This is an element that is still missing from the majority of public dialogues and is perhaps a contribution we have made.

Netanel Miles-Yepez: *I'm curious, what is the difference between the unsatisfying public programs done as part of the Snowmass Conference and the satisfying public programs done in the Spiritual Paths seminars? Ed?*

Edward Bastian: I would say the focus is different. The Snowmass Conference was always meant to be a retreat, and so whenever they attempted to go outside of that they were disappointed. The

Spiritual Paths seminars are *intended* to be public programs, which happen to incorporate some of the retreat aspects of dialogue learned from the Snowmass Conference. Everyone involved knows the focus is on the people attending, so they aren't disappointed.

THE POINTS OF AGREEMENT

Netanel Miles-Yepez: *What was the basis for dialogue after that first session of introductions in 1984?*

Thomas Keating: If our proximate goal was friendship, the ultimate goal was to really understand the religions of the world from the inside, from the perspective of someone who had practiced and benefited from them. And so for several years, maybe the first four years of the Snowmass Conference, we tried to see if we could come up with any agreements on the spiritual level.

We came up with a set of principles that we agreed on, and it was really quite surprising! It wasn't as though there was absolute agreement, but we felt comfortable enough to say "yes" to them, though we might have preferred to express them a little differently here and there. Nevertheless, it does represent a commonality that is very significant and very striking. We called these our "Points of Agreement." I have been asked to publish these in several places. They were even in the "Report" of the World Parliament of Religions that happened in Chicago after the hundred year hiatus.

Netanel Miles-Yepez: *Did you do any work on the "Points of Agreement" in preparation for the first Snowmass Conference in 1984, or did they come solely from the dialogue?*

Thomas Keating: I think there might have been a draft of a few points that we used as a point of departure. Some we threw out right away, and others we worked on. We revised it again the next year and for about four years, total. Then we started discussing our differences. And that was very interesting. But we didn't feel it was necessary to make a list of them.

Tania Leontov: I think I remember Father Tom having drawn up a draft of some "points of agreement" prior to the conference, which he offered to us at the beginning to see if we could agree on them. So that's how we started. I am pretty sure there was one about "God, the Great Mystery," which Pema [Chödrön] and I objected to as Buddhists, really holding out for a long time until the language was finally adjusted. We were willing to talk about "the vast expanse," but not God; it just doesn't work in Buddhism.

You have to remember how new these kinds of dialogues were, and how much we had yet to learn about one another. In time, we got to the point of really enjoying the different perspectives of our traditions.

Robert Dunbar: Yes, it was a struggle for a long time just to come up with a common vocabulary to talk about the "Ultimate Reality" or the "Ultimate Mystery." Many useful discussions hovered around the difference in language between the personal and impersonal systems of thought. We learned very quickly that words had very different meanings and connotations from one tradition to another. So these discussions were very valuable.

Donald Postema: I came in at the tail end of the Points of Agreement discussion, but for me the value in it was an expansion of language. We had to listen hard and discerningly as others spoke of the Ultimate in their own tradition's language just so we could talk together and understand each other. We had to evolve a common language, and it was difficult not using precise words as they are understood in one's own tradition. But as clear as they may be to folks "within the tradition," they may completely mystify folks from other traditions; thus the need to listen and expand one's vocabulary. Our purpose was not to weaken our convictions but to find ways to communicate better.

Netanel Miles-Yepez: *What were some of the "points" that elicited strong reactions? Roger, didn't you mention that it was the "points of agreement" discussion in the first conference that brought you into the group?*

Roger La Borde: Yes, I was an observer that first year, and bit my tongue for a couple of days while the "points" were discussed. My problem was with a point that said, "Daily disciplined meditative practice is *essential* for spiritual awakening." Well, I balked at that one. And when it was agreed that I would be allowed to speak, I said, "I remember this story of a guy named Saul riding his ass down the road. If I remember right, he had a *sudden* awakening, changed his name to Paul, and became a follower of Jesus; somehow, I doubt he was doing daily disciplined meditative practice at that moment. I am guessing that there are a number of other stories in all of the traditions to support spontaneous awakening. Am I right?"

First, Douglas Steere said yes and gave an example. Then, Rami [Shapiro] jumped in with a yes, and we started to go around the circle, each person giving an example of spontaneous awakening from their own tradition! Finally, it came back to me, and I said, "The way I look at this thing about 'daily disciplined meditative practice' goes like this: If you have somebody out on the streets breaking windows and mugging people, getting in all kinds of trouble, and somebody grabs them by the scruff of the neck, pulls them into a gym, and puts boxing gloves on them they can beat up on somebody who wants the same, and it's controlled aggression. But at some point, they tire of the beating and getting beaten and say, "Hey, I don't want to do this anymore." And this is how I view meditation; it keeps you busy 'till you decide to 'wake up,' and the waking up happens in a spontaneous moment; it can happen walking your dog, making love, playing music, or even with a butterfly landing on your nose!"

As it turned out, everybody agreed. So it was changed to, "Daily disciplined meditative practice is *helpful*, but not essential for spiritual awakening." So that was my introduction to the group and a good example of how we worked to refine the "Points of Agreement."

Sudha Puri: I have often read the various revisions of the "Points of Agreement" to my congregation, and they have never failed to blow people away. People just couldn't believe there was so much in common and would say to me, "If only I had known that before! All these traditions have these basic things in common." It was wonderful to see this realization wash over them. This kind of knowledge opens up vistas of inner freedom for people, and allows them to be able to move ahead in their spiritual life, and deepen it, letting go of all the old blockages.

THE DIALOGUE OF DIFFERENCES

Netanel Miles-Yepez: *So, after the "agreements," you turned to the differences; some people would ask, why spend time on these?*

Ibrahim Gamard: We took the differences on very gently. We first focused on what we agreed upon, and as we got to know one another, beginning to trust and feel affection for each other, we started talking about the differences. And there were some difficulties. I had to deal with stereotypes about Islam, and that was difficult for me. So I think it was wise that the differences came up only after the safe environment was established.

Henoch Dov Hoffman: Some people have said, "If we agree on eighty percent of the issues, let's focus on the eighty and not the twenty." But that's not much fun; the dialogue becomes sterile if you are always focused on safe subjects. It becomes inauthentic. It is important to establish commonalities and to share experiences, but if you can't explore your issues in the intimacy of a group like this, what good is the intimacy?

Atmarupananda: Often Hindus are rightly criticized for too glibly saying, "We're all one, and it is all the same." But that's not what

the tradition says; that is just what people say who take a super-
ficial view of the matter. A particular path has its own integrity,
but there are accretions accumulated over time in a tradition that
may not be essential, while other parts are completely integrated.
And unless you understand that, you can't really understand the
experience of another person.

Henoch Dov Hoffman: The milk shake model of recent Western spirituality, where no one has any position, doesn't lead anywhere.
To get a connection, you have to know a difference.

Robert Dunbar: This was an aspect of the dialogue that I really loved.
It was an opportunity to learn something, to acquire an intellectual apprehension of traditions I was not very familiar with. For
instance, when I first became a member, I had had very little exposure to Buddhism, and to Buddhists. In our group we have had
wonderful representatives of both Tibetan Buddhism and Zen
Buddhism. And I have learned so much from each of them.

When Gesshin Prabhasa Dharma Roshi was still alive and
active in our group, I clung to every word she said. I admired her
immensely; she was just such a beautiful spiritual person and
exemplar. I felt I could sit at her feet for a lifetime. With her, I had
the sense that I was always learning something new and important; she just made so much sense to me. And that is one of the
principle things I am always looking for in dialogue, to learn . . .
and also to be inspired as I was by Gesshin.

Netanel Miles-Yepez: *That's an interesting point; this was really a
unique opportunity to learn about other traditions from deep
practitioners; surely it was better than a book?*

Roger La Borde: It was nothing less than a living library of scholars!
When I wanted to know something about Catholicism, I didn't
have to seek it out in the bowels of the Vatican library; I could pick
up the phone and talk to Tom, and say, "Hey, Tom what do you

think about this? Here's my take." I have that with each of my friends from these different traditions, and I think it's incredible.

Henoch Dov Hoffman: It's a gold mine of information. As someone who has always been interested in comparative religion, I find it a dream come true.

Netanel Miles-Yepez: *And you get the benefit of their personal experience.*

Roger La Borde: Sure, because I know they've studied it and come to their own conclusions. Years ago, I asked Tom, "Do you really feel that Jesus lived, was crucified, and later resurrected?" And he basically said to me, "I don't have to derive my belief from history; I have a personal relationship with Jesus." That's another way of saying, "I don't need the book; I know the person."

Sudha Puri: This aspect was tremendous; we got to know every one of these traditions intimately through the Snowmass Conference. That is not to say that we got to know them completely, only that we had a personal experience of them. Every tradition now had a face: the Orthodox Church looked like Father Timko and Father Hopko; Judaism looked like Rami [Shapiro], Dovid Din, Shlomo Schwartz, and Howard [Hoffman]; Islam was Imam Bilal Hyde and Ibrahim Gamard. It is an incredible opportunity to be able to ask questions of people who really know, and to pursue these in group, and during meals, saying, "I really don't understand where you are coming from on this; would you explain it to me a little more?"

Ibrahim Gamard: But I also feel that we have missed an opportunity to learn more. It has been said a number of times that we didn't really need to spend time reading texts about one another's traditions, that we got more out of hearing each other speaking spontaneously from the heart and personal experience. I respect this view, but I also feel it would have been better if people had been more educated about the traditions. I still feel that most members know little about Islam, about the unique teachings and principles of the tradition.

Netanel Miles-Yepez: *So, for you, this is a weakness in the dialogue of differences that could use improvement?*

Ibrahim Gamard: I think it was a weakness that we didn't spend time in between conferences actually learning more of the facts and history of each other's traditions. I understand why, but I still believe we would benefit from it.

Netanel Miles-Yepez: *Why doesn't it happen?*

Ibrahim Gamard: All of us are very busy, and usually think of the conference as a "retreat" from that busyness; so we aren't exactly eager to do more work. Also there is a tendency to completely forget about it all between sessions, like distant friends between visits. Although a few people have developed friendships where they visit each other in between, by and large people show up after a year's separation and are glad to reconnect and to do the work, but haven't really learned anything new. But I would be willing to do that work in between.

Netanel Miles-Yepez: *That's a good point. Were there any other critical differences? And by that I mean differences that were essential, or challenging to work with?*

Atmarupananda: Yes, one was between the personal systems and the impersonal systems. Hinduism, of course, has both the theistic and the nontheistic, but because it has the nontheistic it is easy to speak from an impersonal standpoint. And this is one of the biggest differences that we have had to bridge. Some representatives of the personal systems, for instance, often couldn't understand why things were important to us, and sometimes brushed subtle distinctions aside as irrelevant, feeling that we were making meaningless distinctions. But from the standpoint of an impersonal system, these distinctions are very important.

Netanel Miles-Yepez: *For instance, the difference in language between "one" and "nondual," "monism" in contrast to "nondualism," advaita?*

Atmarupananda: Yes, this was a nonissue to them. To say "one" is a positive statement, and we believe that the best you can do regarding the Absolute Reality is to make a negative statement, saying, "not two."

Roger La Borde: In the Native American tradition, there were also a number of things that our group wanted to discuss that just didn't exist in there. A simple example would be a weed. There is no concept of a "weed" among Native Americans; everything has a purpose, a place.

Netanel Miles-Yepez: *Chicory is not a useless weed! It makes a good tea!*

Roger La Borde: That's right, so we had a number of things like this that came up over the years.

Netanel Miles-Yepez: *I want to come back to something for just a moment. Now, I agree that there is a distinction between impersonal and personal traditions in general, but on another level no tradition is that simple. As Swamiji mentioned, Hinduism has both theistic (personal) and nontheistic (impersonal) traditions, but this is also true in a sense of Christianity, Judaism and Islam. In the Kabbalistic tradition of Judaism, the* Ain Sof *or* Atzmut *is impersonal; in the Sufi tradition,* la illaha ill allah-hu *expresses both the unmanifest and manifest aspects of God; and in the esoteric traditions of Christianity, we have the Godhead, which is impersonal. Likewise, Buddhism also has its own ways of personalizing the Ultimate Reality, whether in sects or in a particular aspect of a practice. So perhaps we should say that on the* *whole there are traditions more embracing of personal language, with regard to speaking about the Ultimate Reality, and others more embracing of impersonal language.*

Tania Leontov: I think this was a consensus generally reached in the group over the years as well.

Netanel Miles-Yepez: *How about you, Father Keating? You said the differences were "interesting," but did you find any value in discussing them?*

Thomas Keating: Yes, I did. But "the dialogue of differences" is not the same with a group that feels at home with each other and can ask almost anything at this point, as we can in the Snowmass Conference. We have a great time. And it is that atmosphere that is crucial to interreligious dialogue on the human level. When you feel at home and in confidence with others, you are not so worried about critical judgments "waiting to catch the ball," so to speak. Rather, it is a valued sharing of a different perspective on a topic. That is the spirit of the group that I would like to see preserved in some way, to serve as a model for others who would like to do this work, and further it.

Along with the differences, we were also taking on various issues, common elements in the way of practice, fasting, spiritual reading, guidance, chanting, trying to lead daily life from a meditative motive, from the contemplative space; all of those things that are common. All of the religions have practices like these, though some emphasize one more than another.

DEEP STRUCTURES

Netanel Miles-Yepez: *In linguistic terminology, you engaged in a synchronic look at the deep structures of your respective traditions—looking at a cross-section of practices or issues from the differing perspectives of your respective traditions?*

Tania Leontov: Yes, and this has pretty much been our main dialogue objective since we worked on the "Points of Agreement." We come up with some topics, and we bring to the table how each of our traditions looks at these things, and then how we personally look at them. For some, this is the only place where they can say what they really believe. And people really open up at meals and on walks, and we learn deeply from seeing this cross-section.

Netanel Miles-Yepez: *How do you come up with the topics?*

Robert Dunbar: We always argue about the agenda. These are very independent people, people who are usually the head of something, so there is always some bargaining that goes on before we finally settle on something. Then as the group goes on, you'll usually find out that it wasn't entirely settled after all. But eventually we agree and get down to business.

Sudha Puri: Having a center near Boston, where the issue of same-sex marriage is so powerful, I asked the question at our last meeting: "What does your tradition teach, and what do you personally believe, about homosexuality and same-sex marriage?" Well, I was blown away by the response, not to mention surprised, when the views I thought would be narrow turned out to be fairly liberal!

So when we get on a really interesting topic, and people start quoting from their sources and bringing real light to the topics, you can't help but come away with a new perspective.

Robert Dunbar: Yes, the homosexuality topic was really a hot potato, but, boy, the group came to life talking about this. We had never really discussed it before, and it was a wonderful session. Everyone really listened, and it worked. This is a big topic in the Episcopal Church right now and in society in general. So I was very happy to get to discuss that. I am always hoping that the dialogue will catch fire, as it did on this topic.

Like Sudha, I was also surprised. I had assumed Orthodox Judaism would take a very hard line on this issue, and while it was not encouraged, they are very tolerant of homosexuality and have an interesting view of it. Rabbi Hoffman is just a marvel. He is a profound scholar and can tell you how something is viewed in Jewish mysticism as well as in rabbinics. I admire his ability to be both open and yet completely adherent to his tradition. He is one of the people I have gotten to know personally the best, especially through discussions like this.

CHAPTER THREE

BASES AND BOUNDARIES

FRIENDSHIP AND TRUST

Netanel Miles-Yepez: *Now I want to get down to talking about the foundations of dialogue—friendship, meditation, the boundary issues, the problems and what keeps you together through the problems. Sudha Ma mentioned that the first session "is where trust was built," and Father Keating said it became the place where friendships were renewed. How important is trust and friendship to this dialogue?*

Henoch Dov Hoffman: Friendship and trust are enormously important if people are going to share over a long period of time. Without it, the dialogue sinks into posturing and the defense of egos, and wastes a lot of time. Friendship just engenders a totally different quality of dialogue.

Netanel Miles-Yepez: *What builds that trust?*

Henoch Dov Hoffman: For me, it is sharing the "shadow" aspects of our traditions and lives; sharing real life and real life problems. Religious leaders are terribly susceptible to expectations of perfection, and it's a burden. As we share more of ourselves as complete human beings, our frustrations and our "burnout" issues through the dialogues, over meals and walks, it builds that necessary trust.

Netanel Miles-Yepez: *Father Keating, was this building of trust and friendship part of the original vision?*

Thomas Keating: From the beginning, I knew we had a better chance of having a true dialogue if we could become friends, but that could not happen if we kept our guard up. So it is a reciprocal process. You need to have the right attitude of openness to come to friendship, but you need the friendship to continue to support the difficult inner work of staying open. For friendship and intimacy to occur, it is really necessary to establish a safe place where people can freely contribute what they have experienced in their own tradition or through particular practices. This was the reason we were disinclined to have any observers at the Snowmass Conference, because what was developing was a kind of friendship that enabled us to feel comfortable and safe enough to share, to disclose to each other, what our own spiritual journey was like, our individual goals, and also to perceive the many common elements that are present both in the practices and the metaphysics. You usually won't tell your secrets to somebody unless you're friends or until you know that person. So the idea of getting acquainted and being at ease in private was a primary goal.

Tania Leontov: Fairly early on, people relaxed completely and became comfortable; there was a lot of teasing, joking, taking someone else's position. A real affection and appreciation grew up among us. It was amazing; we had hardly any contact through the year, but we always picked up so easily.

Robert Dunbar: It would be fascinating to see a sociogram of the dynamics of our dialogues. There have been great friendships that have developed over the years and others that just haven't happened. For whatever reason, some people just have natural affinities for one another, and these people end up speaking more honestly outside of the formal sessions. That's just the way any group dynamic works.

Netanel Miles-Yepez: *Can someone give me an example of a "natural affinity?"*

Roger La Borde: I really had this kind of relationship with Father George Timko, the Eastern Orthodox priest, who has since passed on. What a joy he was! I love that man and always will. We had some heated debates over the years, and he never took it personally. He was like a pit bull; once he got hold of something, he was going to shake until he understood it. I remember at the second conference in La Crescenta, we were up till two or three in the morning, two nights in a row, in heated debate. I think we were arguing about the existence of absolute Good and absolute Evil. We fought that out back and forth for a long time before we finally came to a resolution. But there was no stopping him once he had got hold of it!

I watched him and our relationship change so quickly and move so deeply; it had nothing to do with theology or dogmas and everything to do with energy and spirit and genuine joy in being with each other.

Ibrahim Gamard: I remember when I first entered the conference, George really pushed me on some issues, and I was a little uncomfortable with it. But then somebody came to me and said, "The way to be friends with George is to debate with him." So I started to engage him, and he became more and more affectionate toward me. I was amazed; he even took my wife and me out to lunch, and he was very kind to her. So this to me is a clear example of how to work with different personality types in the sociogram of dialogue.

Edward Bastian: I didn't meet George until 1999, but I had a very different initial encounter with him. During our first morning meditation together, I ended up having a powerful spiritual experience. Because I was writing a book on spiritual methodologies and experiences, I wanted to talk about it. But this is something that usually isn't done, as it often opens the situation to a lot of ego posturing. Nevertheless, I felt comfortable in that atmosphere, and decided to open up about my experience. And as I did, right across the room, facing me in the circle, was George. Our

eyes met, and he said, "Ed, that sounds exactly like the experience brought about by the *hesychast* meditation of the Eastern
Orthodox Church."

Years before, my brother Ken had introduced me to a crusty
old iconoclastic political science professor named Hube Wilson.
He was a very interesting person, and we liked him a lot. So once,
as a joke, we asked him what his religion was, thinking we would
get a little taste of his sardonic wit. But he answered us straight,
saying, "I'm a *hesychast*." At the time, we weren't sure if we had
not gotten the joke, or if it was just something he had made up.
But I never forgot that word. Here I was, all these years later,
hearing the same word again from George with regard to my
own meditation experience! What George told me led me to
really dig into reading about the *hesychast* tradition, and it was
this shared experience and knowledge that formed an immediate
bond between us.

Henoch Dov Hoffman: I don't think we can overestimate the value
of shared experience when it comes to friendship in a group like
this. Ibrahim can tell you a good story about our own friendship
in this regard.

Netanel Miles-Yepez: *How about it, Ibrahim?*

Ibrahim Gamard: When Howard [Henoch Dov] was invited to
attend his first conference in 1995, he and I were chatting
between sessions about our mutual love for the beauty of the
mountains around Snowmass. And he told me about how he was
trying to combine a group counseling process with mountaineer-
ing, somewhat in the manner of the Outward Bound program for
youth. Hearing that, I casually mentioned that I had been in the
Colorado Outward Bound School when I was sixteen. Then
Howard said, "Oh! I was in the Colorado Outward Bound
School!" "What year?" I asked. "1963." "Which course were
you in?" "The second course." With more than a little surprise,
I said, "I was in the second course!" Then he asked me, "Who
was your squad leader?" And I answered, "I think he was

Australian." He said the name, and I replied with a big smile, "Yes! That's him."

Thirty-two years before, we were in the same squad of the Colorado Outward Bound School and had climbed three "four-teeners" [14,000-foot mountains] in three days together and even camped overnight together on top of South Maroon Peak. We were both sixteen! During the next two days of that trip, we also climbed Capital Peak and Mount Snowmass. I distinctly remember, as we came down the other side of Mount Snowmass, looking at my map and seeing a little black square that said "St. Benedict's Monastery!" And here we were, together again, at Snowmass, thirty-two years later!

We started laughing and hugging like two long-lost friends, like we had fallen in love. Within seconds, people were coming up and asking, "What's happened with you two, you look like long-lost friends!" Needless to say, that meeting and what we had shared all those years before formed a real bond for us.

Netanel Miles-Yepez: *That's an incredible story.*

Henoch Dov Hoffman: I think Ibrahim and I are technically the first members of the Snowmass Conference, or at least we have the most seniority.

Netanel Miles-Yepez: *Granted!*

THE SILENT DIALOGUE

Netanel Miles-Yepez: *I was interested in something Sudha Ma mentioned earlier—namely that "the dialogue of the Snowmass Conference relies on a common experience of contemplative depth." How was this "common experience" developed?*

Roger La Borde: It was decided early on that the one ritual discourse we all had in common, and that all of us could do together as a ceremony, was to sit in silence.

Henoch Dov Hoffman: People get along a lot better when they don't open their mouths. I am joking, of course, but there is a unity in that silence that the silence makes possible. And it has a profound effect; connections happen in the silence that couldn't happen any other way.

Netanel Miles-Yepez: *And how often would you do this?*

Sudha Puri: We meditated in silence together twice a day, each day, for an hour at a time, usually before breakfast and supper.

Netanel Miles-Yepez: *How does sharing this silence affect the group? Ed?*

Edward Bastian: If you threw a bunch of angry people in a room together, they wouldn't have to say anything to one another for the anger to be communicated and shared. They are already tuned to the same frequency. Now imagine a room full of experienced meditators sitting in silence with one another, tuning into the sacred dimension as each of them knows it. Both groups of people might have silence, but what is communicated is going to be quite different. In my own experience, something profound is shared in that meditative "space." If individual consciousness is noncorporeal, and if in meditation we share an intention, isn't it possible that consciousness fuses and a larger group consciousness is formed? In that environment, on that level, the boundary lines of consciousness break down. And what follows that kind of sharing is different.

In meditation circles, we often use the phrase "holding the space," saying he or she is "holding the space." In some ways, we rely on our senior members for that, our wisdom holders, like Father Keating. An experienced meditator can enter that state, and that consciousness then begins to pervade the atmosphere, and others can tune in to that. But a group of skilled meditators can do it simultaneously, and a merging of consciousness happens more spontaneously. But in the beginning you really need Father Keating or a Gayatri Devi to do that for you.

Ibrahim Gamard: I agree. I can still remember how palpable Gayatri Devi's presence was during the silent meditation.

Donald Postema: There was truly a profound connection without words. And I remember that during one of those silent sessions in Cohasset, I had a profound experience of the Presence of Jesus; my own experience of Christianity was strengthened through sharing meditation with folks of different spiritual traditions!

Netanel Miles-Yepez: *So if you turn to dialogue after this shared experience, what is the impact on the dialogue?*

Edward Bastian: It changes they way you talk about things. It isn't a conscious change, but the words and thoughts just seem to come from a deeper level. You can hear the difference when someone is speaking from contemplative depth, as opposed to when they are speaking from a more mundane "set." That meditative intentionality is like a subtle dye infusing group consciousness and affecting the quality of discourse.

Netanel Miles-Yepez: *Is this done as a ritual to open a session of formal dialogue?*

Edward Bastian: No, it isn't, but I think it should be. For me, the silent meditation is the heart of the retreat, and I think we should do more of it; a short session just before beginning a formal dialogue, and perhaps another in the middle of the day sometime. People are together talking all the time during the conference, and I think there needs to be a little more time for individual reflection, just to process all of the information coming at you. Meditation is the centerpiece of the Snowmass Conference for me, the source from which all else flows.

CENTERING PRAYER AND DIALOGUE

Netanel Miles-Yepez: *If it's all right with everyone, I'd like to turn to Father Keating for a moment. Father Keating, is there a relationship between deep meditative experience and the ability to dialogue effectively? After all, the two foci of your spiritual leadership in the last thirty years have been the Centering Prayer movement and the Snowmass Conference.*

Thomas Keating: I think this is true for me personally. The Centering Prayer work began around 1976 at St. Joseph's Abbey, after a year's trial of a method by Father William Meninger, basing himself on indications from *The Cloud of Unknowing*. But I wasn't expecting to continue with that work after I resigned as abbot in 1981. I was hoping to focus on dialogue. Nevertheless, I became more and more involved with the Centering Prayer movement over time, and this eventually grew into Contemplative Outreach at the end of 1984. So there has been something of a tension for me in trying to serve both categories, both ecumenism and Contemplative Outreach.

Netanel Miles-Yepez: *Really? When I have observed you in interreligious dialogue or teaching Centering Prayer, you seem to move seamlessly from one category to the other, almost as if there was an intrinsic relationship between the two.*

Thomas Keating: Yes, there was a lot of interaction between the two, and it has grown over the years. It was all evolving at that time. You see, a great many Christians had joined one or another of the Eastern disciplines over the years because they couldn't find any spirituality in the Christian milieu, whether in churches, parishes, or schools; in fact, many have said to me that, had they known there was a Christian contemplative practice, they wouldn't have gone to the East. But still, I think they have benefited by it, and many have remained there. Others, however, have returned to the religion of their childhood because they really felt more at home there. And so, with a practice that was comparable to what they had learned in Buddhism or Sikhism, they were able to continue their journey in continuity with the religion of their youth.

But that was not our reason for doing this work. The point was really just to renew the Christian contemplative tradition, and to make it an option in the marketplace for those who would never have the opportunity, or who would not go through the difficulty of learning the comprehensive and integrated wisdom of those teachings.

Netanel Miles-Yepez: *Why did you feel this was a need?*

Thomas Keating: During my early encounters with teachers of other traditions at St. Joseph's Abbey, I met a lot of Buddhist and Hindu teachers and their students, and it was evident to me that they were benefiting from their practices. For example, there was a psychospiritual wisdom presented in the form of methods articulated in Buddhist meditative disciplines that wasn't articulated in quite the same detailed and practical way in the Christian scheme of things. Certainly these existed in the Christian tradition, but they were fairly diffuse and not quite so focused on a practical daily method with comparable psychological insights. It was as if these teachers and their students had arrived at the monastery, saying, "Here's our method; what's yours?" And there was no answer; we really didn't have a method as clearly articulated as theirs.

For us, the monastic lifestyle was a structure, an environment conducive to spirituality, but it wasn't a method in the same sense. It certainly had many practical rules and disciplines, many of which are duplicated in almost all monastic traditions, but they didn't quite apply to the individual in the same way that many of the Buddhist practices did. For instance, consider mantra recitation from the Hindu and Buddhist traditions; this was present in the Christian tradition, but was not as well worked out or directly applied to the individual—based on the individual's needs, temperament and personality—as seemed to be the case in Eastern spiritual traditions.

Netanel Miles-Yepez: *It seems to me, looking back over your career and your writings, that you have spent a great deal of time and energy not only articulating a clear "method," but also making the psychological and contemplative sophistication of Christianity explicit.*

Thomas Keating: That's true. It was there, but it was distributed over a great number of books. In this work, I benefited a great deal from contemporary science and psychology, especially from developmental psychology, which I feel is an essential kind of truth that all of the world's traditions need to take into account. Likewise, I believe that the teaching about the unconscious, from Freud onward, has had tremendous consequences for the spiritual journey.

Netanel Miles-Yepez: *Do you see this development in your work as an outgrowth of those early dialogues with Buddhists?*

Thomas Keating: Yes and no. Keep in mind, I was teaching the contemplative dimension of the Gospel from the time I became Novice Master in 1954, and some of my books, like *Crisis of Faith, Crisis of Love*, are conferences that I gave to novices in the early 1950s, and these I later modified and presented to the community when I became abbot in 1961.

Netanel Miles-Yepez: *I feel there is a subtle move that happened historically that will probably be overlooked in the history of interspiritual dialogue because the bridge is so short. When Zen and Tibetan Buddhism arrived on the American scene, it was their meditation that was drawing people initially. And it seems to me that there was also a ferment and parallel interest in reviving the contemplative aspects of the Abrahamic traditions in the mid- to late 1950s; it was happening at the same time with you, with Rabbi Zalman Schachter-Shalomi, and with Father Thomas Merton. This interest and activity very narrowly preceded the interest in interfaith dialogue. Perhaps there is a relationship between the two—an attempt to talk about the tools of the trade? Is it possible that the growth that was happening in that* *sphere fueled and followed into what became a dialogical movement?*

Thomas Keating: Yes, there is no doubt that there was a movement of the Holy Spirit to revive those things at the same time. And that was partially due to the accessibility and interpenetration of different cultures.

One of Sasaki Roshi's students, Leonard Cohen, was the first person to tell me about the Hasidic mystical tradition of Judaism that was present in Poland, which was virtually destroyed in the Holocaust. He told me that he would have been a part of that tradition if it was still accessible, but instead he hooked up with Sasaki Roshi. Later, I met Rabbi Dovid Din, Rabbi Zalman Schachter-Shalomi, and his successor at Naropa University, Rabbi Miles Krassen—all of whom were continuing this mystical tradition and making its contemplative depths available to people.

Netanel Miles-Yepez: *I think that helps to shed a little more light on the subject.*

RITUAL AND BOUNDARIES

Netanel Miles-Yepez: *I'm wondering how you shared in the experience of one another's rituals.*

Atmarupananda: When I first came into the group, I was asked to do a *puja* to the sacred forms—God, Allah, Brahman—because formal recognition of the sacred is very important to establishing the sacredness of the dialogue itself.

Tania Leontov: This may not be the most significant ritual we shared, but when Gerald Red Elk was with us we liked to have him do our mealtime prayers. His prayer was so heartfelt; he would stand there with tears the size of grapes coming from his eyes, totally comfortable showing his devotion so openly and praying from the depth of his soul. It was very inspiring to me, personally.

Netanel Miles-Yepez: *Were there any other more formal rituals performed?*

Sudha Puri: Oh sure, we've done a fair amount of this over the years, and I have always enjoyed sharing ritual as well as participating in the liturgies of the place we were staying. When Ibrahim demonstrated the whirling of the Mevlevi dervishes, it was so beautiful (though when he tried to instruct us, we were like wobbly tops). Likewise, Gesshin Prabhasa Dharma Roshi taught us walking meditation, Father Thomas instructed us in Centering Prayer, Mataji sang Tagore songs, and we celebrated the Sabbath with our rabbis. It was a wonderful experience.

Tania Leontov: At this last meeting, we got a little more playful, going from singing camp songs to chanting mantras!

Donald Postema: I found that one way to really "know" someone's spirituality is to share in that person's rituals or worship. I have long had a real love for Gregorian chant and Catholic liturgy, so it was no surprise that attending Mass and other liturgies at St. Benedict's Monastery gave me a unique insight into Father Thomas's spiritual life. But I was surprised to find similarities between the Native American pipe ceremony and the Holy Communion of Christians.

Netanel Miles-Yepez: *When I spoke to Jim Barnett [formerly **Swami Buddhananda**], he told me that the Native American pipe ceremony was one of the most universally accepted of the shared rituals, and that even Gayatri Devi, whose rules of purity would usually prevent her from participating in such a ritual, also took up the pipe. Afterward, she asked him, "Baba, did I do right?" And he answered her, "You did wonderful." He felt she was more courageous in doing this than most swamis would be.*

Tania Leontov: Gayatri Devi was an exceptional person and I think instinctively understood that the situation transcended the ordinary commitments.

Netanel Miles-Yepez: *In the same conversation, Jim also mentioned to me that, in the first or second year, he, Father Keating, Rami Shapiro and Bilal Hyde were all invited over to the Lama Foundation in New Mexico to share rituals with the people there. He said everyone participated, and that it was a big hit with both the "clergy" and the participants.*

Tania Leontov: I think the ritual sharing was helpful in the sense of offering insight; you get to see what the practices are aiming for and how they help people connect with something vaster than themselves. But there were also people who found it difficult to participate in some of these rituals. So, for the most part, we stuck to silent meditation; stilling the mind is part of many different traditions.

Netanel Miles-Yepez: *What were the difficulties?*

Atmarupananda: When I did the Hindu *puja*, I included everybody, but the actual inclusion was problematic for some. By including the name of God recognized in Judaism or Islam among other names, it could be construed as if I was suggesting that these were merely deities among other deities, which is anathema in those traditions. This is not how the *puja* is conceived in my tradition, but the perception was the issue. So while I found it highly beneficial when others shared their rituals, it wasn't a universally appreciated activity.

Henoch Dov Hoffman: Yes, the concept of God's oneness in Judaism is protected by a "fence" of *halakhah*, or legal requirements, that will not allow us to associate with what may even be *perceived* as idolatry by a bystander, even when it is not. This was one reason I preferred the silent meditation. It was the easiest group ritual for me to participate in, as it didn't conflict with any of my commitments as an Orthodox Jew.

Ibrahim Gamard: I remember a similar issue with the peace pipe ceremony. Rabbi Shlomo Schwartz felt he could not participate in this, because it had an idolatrous association, and I felt a kinship with him on this issue and wanted to support him. It was funny; I think some of the earlier rabbis looked at me with uneasiness because I am a Muslim, perhaps wary that I was anti-Jewish or something, but during the dialogues, time and time again, we found ourselves allied on many of the same points. We decided not to join in the peace pipe ceremony, and that was completely accepted by the group.

COMMITMENTS

Netanel Miles-Yepez: *This is an interesting issue to pursue. Now that I think about it, at least Ibrahim and Reb Henoch Dov must have had a number of boundary challenges in this environment; is that right? What about the crucifixes, Reb Henoch Dov?*

Henoch Dov Hoffman: Going into a Church is always a problem. When I go into my room at the monastery, I put the crucifixes away. When Roger [La Borde] discovered this, he went ahead and covered up the crucifix in the chapel. I was hesitant even to ask about that . . . my room is one thing, but the chapel is something else entirely. I really appreciated his doing that for me.

I have always been fond of the monastic chanting of the psalms, and this even inspired me to set up a service where we chant all the psalms three times a week. But I wouldn't go to a church to pray; I can go to a mosque, but it is simply forbidden for us to pray in proximity to icons and crucifixes.

Netanel Miles-Yepez: *Now we know one another, and I know the answer to this next question, but I think it will be good to clarify this a little further for people who are not familiar with Orthodox*

Judaism. Is it an issue of conscience, honoring the rules of the tradition, or a personal disdain for iconography for you?

Henoch Dov Hoffman: The rules of the tradition are very clear and very strict regarding what are, by definition, "idols" and representations of divinity. These are to be avoided whenever possible. Rabbi Moshe ben Maimon, known as Maimonides to philosophers, spells this out very clearly: a Jew is permitted to pray in a mosque, but not in a church. So it is ensconced in *halakhah*, the Jewish legal tradition, that even being around what is perceived to be an idol is forbidden; even having a tangential connection with it is to be avoided.

It was a delicate moment for me regarding the crucifix in the chapel, and I didn't want to offend Father Thomas regarding it, so I was sitting there debating what to do when Roger came to my rescue. And the interesting thing was that Roger did it without any compunction whatsoever! Nobody said a word about it, even though it was covered for several days. I was so worried about that; Jewish self-consciousness, I suppose. So we do have commitments to honor, even with the utmost respect for other traditions.

Netanel Miles-Yepez: *Ibrahim, how did you work around having to do the five-times-a-day prayer of* salat *while at the Snowmass Conference? After all, the schedule was pretty full.*

Ibrahim Gamard: It wasn't much of a problem. First of all, there is a lenience for travelers; you do two instead of four sets of prostrations for most of the prayers, and you can combine the two afternoon prayers and the two evening prayers. I would set my watch alarm for the predawn prayer, and then would go back to sleep until about an hour before breakfast time. Then I did the noon prayer easily after lunch, and the late afternoon prayer any time before sunset. The sun set just after dinner, and I recall one time joining in some discussion at the diner table after eating, then walking down to the meditation room of the guest building to do the sunset prayer, and then returned to my seat at the table.

In Islam, there are periods when the prayers are due. At this last conference, there was about an hour from the earliest sign of dawn until sunrise, about three and a half hours for the noon prayer, just less than three hours for the second afternoon prayer, just over an hour for the sunset prayer, and four or more hours for the late evening prayer. The middle times—when the "Call to Prayer" is recited from the minarets of mosques in Muslim countries—are considered best (except for the sunset prayer, which is best done very soon), but one can pray any time during the period. And if one misses a prayer during its period, then the prayer can be made up—preferably before bedtime (my rule, such as during my job when I miss a prayer).

Netanel Miles-Yepez: *And, Reb Henoch Dov, how were your prayer obligations accommodated?*

Henoch Dov Hoffman: My needs were always met with sensitivity. I simply took the time I needed to *davven* [pray] on Shabbat, and everyone just accepted it. The food issue was more complicated. I bought some special items, and I also spoke to the cook beforehand about buying food with a *heksher*, a kosher seal of approval.

Netanel Miles-Yepez: *I think many people find your openness and strict adherence to tradition an odd mix—refreshing, but odd. How do you explain it?*

Henoch Dov Hoffman: The idea of the *hasid* is that one is increasingly strict about one's own personal practice, while becoming a more and more warm and flexible person toward others. I know, the usual example is more rigid, less tolerant. But it was the innovation of the Ba'al Shem Tov, who founded Hasidism, to stand this on its end.

Netanel Miles-Yepez: *In Judaism, there is the* mitnagged, *"the opponent," who is observant of the law and intolerant, and the* hasid *who is observant and more tolerant. What makes the difference?*

What keeps the hasid *from falling into the trap of intolerance as a result of increased personal strictness?*

Henoch Dov Hoffman: It is expressed by the Ba'al Shem Tov's saying, "Humility, separation and sweetening unity." The idea of making boundaries is to create integrity; clarification is vital, and if you do that based on humility, then there will be a unity with whatever you are separating from. Whether it is milk and meat, women and men, Catholics and Jews, the result of the separation will be a unification. I would call it the clarifying separation. I believe in that. If it is done with arrogance, on the other hand, the result of the separation will be blame and shame and more conflict.

Netanel Miles-Yepez: *Swami Atmarupananda, I am wondering how you deal with commitment in an order as openly ecumenical as the Ramakrishna Order? Did you find the possibilities distracting, or did you find yourself needing to become more grounded in that tradition?*

Atmarupananda: When I first joined the order, though I loved the Vedanta philosophy I had been studying Chinese Buddhism for a while, and for the first several years I was in the order I felt culturally more akin to things Chinese. I had even studied Chinese and kept my Chinese texts with me in the monastery, and this became a real conflict for me for several years. As if that weren't enough, I also developed a great love for Catholic and Eastern Orthodox mysticism and monasticism. So all of these traditions were pulling at me, and I didn't know precisely where I belonged—"Vedanta is wonderful, but . . . what if . . .?"

After five years in the order, I went to India to stay for seven years. The first two of these years in India I spent in our training college at our headquarters. I studied Sanskrit and the scriptures and enjoyed it immensely, but still I kept my Chinese-language books, which I had not been able to pursue for some time. But I still had the idea that I would. And when I did papers in the training college, if they were to be on religious thinkers other than persons in my lineage, instead of picking thinkers in the Hindu tradition, I would pick Nagarjuna, the great Indian Buddhist philosopher, and Wang-Fo, the Chinese Zen teacher. So that interest was still very active and the source of a mild conflict.

When I finished the training college, I was going by taxi to Calcutta and suddenly there was a very clear moment when I realized that some of my deep psychological structures had shifted. It had been years in the making, but I suddenly saw it; my identity was now completely rooted in Vedanta; my spiritual identity had solidified in this tradition. It was a striking experience, and I can still remember it quite clearly. After that, I gave away my Chinese books; I no longer needed to keep that secret option open. I continued to love and respect Buddhism and Christianity, but now it was from the standpoint of Vedanta. I no longer felt a conflict as to where I actually belonged. So that was an important shift in my internal life.

Netanel Miles-Yepez: *Would you say that being rooted in the tradition, and knowing it, heightened and clarified your approach to ecumenism?*

Atmarupananda: Very much so. One of the riches we have today (never possible before) is access to all of the world's spiritual traditions. In any metropolitan area are teachers of almost every tradition you can think of; and even in small towns there are bookstores and libraries with books on these traditions. The downside is that, with so many choices, often one cannot settle on the one tradition most appropriate to oneself, choosing instead to remain an eternal seeker, never finding a tradition and deepening within it. It is possible to incorporate into one's spiritual life ideas from various traditions, but in my experience this can be done helpfully and healthily only if we are rooted in a particular tradition and practice, taking wisdom from the borders and incorporating them into our center. If we don't have a center, however, but just little bits from here and there, we're not really going anywhere with anything. So we have to have depth and a place to access profundity; that is our tradition and practice within that tradition.

After my experience of becoming rooted in Vedanta, I could understand the depths of other traditions because I understood the depths of my own. I could then assimilate wisdom from elsewhere into my own practice. But before becoming rooted, there was internal conflict (and competition). It was like trying to go east, west, north, and south all at the same time and always feeling a little disoriented. Afterward, I knew I was going north, but could turn and take in the beauty of east, west, and south, and then continue on my journey north. In the end (and here is where the directional analogy fails), all of these paths end in the same place, but you have to walk one to get to that "place" of depth.

MODELS OF DIALOGUE FROM OUR TRADITIONS

Netanel Miles-Yepez: *All of this causes me to wonder, what road do we take to get to the dialogue? What models do we have in our traditions for this? Reb Henoch Dov mentioned one in the Ba'al Shem Tov; are there others that were important to you? Father Keating?*

Thomas Keating: When I started, there weren't many Roman Catholics involved in interfaith dialogue. Thomas Merton was really pushing the boundaries writing about Zen. So he was definitely a pioneer in East–West dialogue.

Netanel Miles-Yepez: *Was his an important example for you?*

Thomas Keating: I had read Merton's books and had even seen some of his unpublished conferences from that time. But really it was the documents of the Second Vatican Council that eventually opened up this possibility for me. At that time, most of the Christian traditions wouldn't touch the Eastern religions with a ten-foot pole! So there wasn't much incentive to study that material, and it was looked upon with a certain hesitation, because it was thought that it might injure the Christian faith. Everybody had a different perspective, but often those perspectives were car- icatured and misrepresented by ignorance and anxiety about the purity of doctrine.

The Second Vatican Council made a 180-degree turn in its attitude, and one particular document of the council spoke specifically about ecumenism with both Christian denominations *and* non-Christian religions. So those documents were liberating, in that they gave people the freedom to pursue this possibility openly. I certainly experienced freedom! And I might never have done so, otherwise. You see, I felt a great loyalty to the Christian scheme of things, and never wanted to dilute the faith in any way for those whom I was trying to encourage in the contemplative lifestyle and in pursuing the spiritual implications of the creed and the major doctrines of the Christian religion. So it was really an enormous change and a step forward, and very few people were prepared for it.

What came first was some dialogue with the other Christian traditions, as there was obviously more in common with them. So, when I started getting interested in interreligious dialogue in the late sixties and meeting some of these teachers, this was brand-new territory and not looked upon with great confidence by some members of the community that I was leading. In other words, you had to move with a certain discretion in these areas. When Sasaki Roshi put on the Cistercian habit and joined us in the refectory, it was a little shocking to some people, and they wondered where in the heck we were going with the monastery.

After the Second Vatican Council, a group called the North American Board of East–West Dialogue was formed. The initia- tive for this group came from one of the congregations at the Vatican, the Congregation for Interreligious Dialogue. Thinking that Benedictine monks and nuns were the logical people to engage in a dialogue with the monks of other traditions (given that both were interested in spirituality and a lifestyle that sup- ported it), Cardinal Pignadoli approached the Abbot General of the Benedictine Order about this possibility; and because we Cistercians were of the same family, so to speak, we were also

invited to take part in this East–West dialogue. That first meeting was held at Petersham, Massachusetts, in 1979, and a board
of trustees was put together. It took a while for the group to be
well accepted in the larger Benedictine community, but even at
that first meeting we had quite a spectrum of people who showed
interest in it, including some Cistercian abbots, one of whom was
me. Other participants were Robert Muller of the United
Nations, Juliet Hollister, Swami Satchidananda, Father Basil
Pennington, Brother David Steindl-Rast, and Raimundo
Panikkar.

Netanel Miles-Yepez: *What was it about this group or this time in
your life that really opened things up in terms of dialogue?*

Thomas Keating: Really it was the time. When I was abbot, as much
as I felt we benefited from these encounters, not all of the monks
were interested. And as abbot, with all the work that office
involved, I couldn't really attend interfaith dialogues as much as,
say, Brother David Steindl-Rast, who was one of the pioneers in
the New York area, especially in his dialogues with Eido Roshi.
I really didn't have time to devote to interreligious dialogues until
I resigned as abbot of St. Joseph's in 1981.

Netanel Miles-Yepez: *After you resigned as abbot in 1981, what
direction did you take?*

Thomas Keating: One thing leads to another. Jacob Needleman had
visited St. Joseph's at one time (I think the first chapter in his book
Lost Christianity describes his visit there) and later invited me to
give a talk in San Francisco to his group. While I was there, I also
gave a talk to a Gurdjieff group, and that summer, I think, I went
to the Naropa Institute to take part in the Buddhist–Christian dialogue initiated by Chögyam Trungpa Rinpoche.
    Later, in the fall, I went to Omega in Rhinebeck, New York,
where there was an interreligious group that included a number
of outstanding people: Rabbi Dovid Din, a fabulous interpreter
of the Hebrew Bible with whom I became close friends, and the

Korean Zen master, Soen Sa Nim, who started a big place in Providence, Rhode Island. He was delightful. He invited me to make a tour of South Korea with him, but I wasn't free to do that at the time. It was shortly after that conference that I convened the Snowmass Conference.

Netanel Miles-Yepez: *Were there other models you looked to, Reb Henoch Dov, outside of the Ba'al Shem Tov, personal or historical?*

Henoch Dov Hoffman: My two teachers in the Hasidic tradition, Rabbi Shloime Twerski of Denver and Rabbi Shlomo Carlebach, were both unusually open for their time. Rabbi Twerski was a Hasidic rabbi of the strictest standards, but he had a philosophy degree from the University of Chicago—very unusual for a Hasidic rebbe—and also had contacts with people of many different traditions. I don't know that he had done any dialogue in the way we do it in the Snowmass Conference, but he was quite open in his way. Reb Shlomo Carlebach was also very encouraging of dialogue and engaged in a rich dialogue with other religions in his lifetime.

But just as important for me have been the many wonderful contacts I have had with people of different faiths over the years. No less important in my intellectual life were the discussions held from day one with Jewish Christians in "Houses of Disputation," as the Talmud calls them. They were rather more on the side of debates than dialogues, but they were still models of the possibility of dialogue.

Then, down through time, many debates, usually staged by the Catholic Church, were held in which Jews and Christians would debate the strengths of their traditions. Most notable among them was the one between Pablo Christiani and Moshe ben Nachman, Nachmanides. This dialogue has stimulated my imagination for many years. So while it is not much, there is some tradition of dialogue.

Netanel Miles-Yepez: *But those disputations weren't very fair to the Jews; on the one hand, the Jews didn't want to make themselves* *look bad and dishonor their own tradition, but neither could they make the Christians look bad, given that the Jews were a small minority in Christian lands.*

Henoch Dov Hoffman: This is true, but I think the earliest dialogues were fair. Only later did they become precarious for Jews. Actually, Nachmanides won that debate, but he had to leave Spain (at the Pope's direction) after doing so. Nevertheless, the king of Spain was interested in the outcome and gave Nachmanides a gift of money for winning. So it wasn't unheard of that Jews won these debates.

Netanel Miles-Yepez: *How about you, Don? Was ecumenism dealt with in Reformed Christianity?*

Donald Postema: Our tradition has a history of relating to plenty of other folks in the Reformed and Evangelical Christian traditions, but our official relations do not extend much beyond other Christian denominations, let alone to other world religions. To tell the truth, that attitude influenced me for a long time. However, working for thirty-four years on the campus of a major university convinced me that religious leaders had to work together if they were to have any influence at all on the university. Meeting and working together gradually broadened my acquaintance with other people of faith, and being part of the Snowmass Conference expanded and deepened my commitment to interfaith dialogue.

Netanel Miles-Yepez: *In the Ramakrishna Order, Swamiji, there is an open door to interspiritual dialogue through Ramakrishna Paramahamsa, because of his own personal engagement with other spiritual traditions; would you tell us something about his dialogue and how it affects members of the order to have his example?*

Atmarupananda: Most people involved in religion come into a particular tradition and follow that path through a lifetime. For

most of us, it takes a lifetime of dedication to make any significant progress on the path, while others may go the length of the
path and come to a state of illumination, staying in that light
until the body finishes its participation in this life. Now, illumination is conceived of differently in different traditions, but there
is usually a relatively straight trajectory through a path to its cul-
mination point. And this is how Ramakrishna started out. He
was born into the Brahmin caste in India and followed a particular path within Hinduism throughout his youth. But after having a life-altering vision of the Divine Mother, he attained
illumination and became curious as to how illumination happened in other paths. So he began to follow different trajectories
within Hinduism, in each case attaining to illumination. He did
this over and over in Hinduism, and then turned to paths in other
religions.

It should be stressed that Ramakrishna wasn't a synthesizer,
using bits of different traditions and putting them together; his
way was to follow a particular path, in its detailed integrity, until
he came to the illumination of that path. For instance, when he
followed Islam, he took a Sufi *pir* [lit. "elder," or master] as a
teacher and lived as a Muslim, performing *salat* ["prayer"] five
times a day until he had attained illumination. And though he
never had a Christian teacher, he read the Christian scriptures
daily with a devotee until he had an experience of Jesus and,
through Jesus, an experience of God in the personal and impersonal aspects—what would be called the "Godhead" in the
Christian tradition. So in his own life he tested different traditions and came to the conclusion that all spiritual paths lead to
the experience of God, or Reality. No matter what their differences are, they are experiencing the same Reality in different
aspects or expressions.

This is a conclusion wholly consistent with the Hindu tradition but, as far as we know, one that had never been proven
before in direct experience the way Ramakrishna proved it. So
this teaching is at the core of the Ramakrishna, or Vedanta, tradition: the belief that all spiritual paths lead to Reality, personal
or impersonal. This affects the tradition and its adherents, open-

ing one first to the value of other traditions and then to the value of dialogue itself. Nevertheless, this example doesn't mean that every devotee of Ramakrishna or monk of the order is actively involved in ecumenism or interreligious dialogue, but it does mean that it is an integral, respected part of the tradition that everyone is aware of, thus open to anyone who wants to participate in it.

Netanel Miles-Yepez: *Was this ecumenical feature important in your own introduction to the order?*

Atmarupananda: For me, it was critical; it was what attracted me to the order. I was brought up in a Protestant Christian home, going to church every Sunday, and I was involved in all manner of church activities, including the choir and youth group. But one day, when I was sixteen, I was standing outside of church waiting for the service to begin after Sunday school, and suddenly a whole flood of ideas came to me:

> We Christians know that Christianity is the only true religion, and we Protestants know that Protestantism is the only true form of Christianity, and my particular denomination, while believing most of the Protestants are good, certainly knows it is the best of the Protestants. So how was it, out of the billions of people in the world, I was one of the lucky few born into the best denomination of the only true half of the only true religion? If the world was created by God, as we were taught, and God was benevolent, why did He appoint me to be so fortunate?
>
> Now, my Catholic friends also believe that Christianity is the only true religion, but regard Catholicism as the only true half of that tradition. So, if I had been born in Saudi Arabia, perhaps I would have grown up thinking that Islam was the only true religion, and my sect of Islam the best form of that religion. And if China (these are the very places and traditions I thought of then) in a Buddhist family, I would think that Buddhism is the only true religion,

and my sect of Buddhism the best form of Buddhism. So it seems to depend on where you are born what you think is true religiously. They teach different things, so they can't all be true; they contradict each other in their exclusive claims, and so, it is most likely that none of them is true.

There on the spot I became an agnostic. Shortly after that, I went to Sweden as an exchange student and came across an English book in a Swedish bookstore. It was called *Vedanta for the Western World*, and on the back cover it said, "Vedanta respects all religious traditions. It believes that all religions are true and that sectarianism [the claim to be exclusively true] is harmful. Religions are different because of the different cultures in which they arose, speaking different languages and having different rituals for different types of people, but all lead to the experience of spiritual Reality." Here was a tradition that had looked at the same evidence I had, and where I came to a negative conclusion, they had come to a positive conclusion. They are all true; it is just the exclusivist claim that is untrue. The language and forms were the expression of it and were different, but not the essence. I felt drawn to this positive conclusion, so I bought the book, took it home to the place I was living, and everything that I read in it seemed to ring true with something inside of me.

Netanel Miles-Yepez: *Were there models for you to follow, Ibrahim?*

Ibrahim Gamard: I have had for most of my life a great appreciation for the mystical traditions of different traditions, and I studied a variety of these in college. But within Islam there is a basic ecumenical tenet that says, "A Muslim is not to denounce another Muslim as an unbeliever over differences of opinion." This is a very old example of tolerance, and one that I think can be expanded to accommodate ecumenism as we see it today. The Mevlevi Sufi order, which I belong to, is also famous for tolerance. We are strict only toward our own egos, which is very similar to what Howard [Henoch Dov] was saying earlier. In this regard, the Mevlevi Order is similar to the famous Chishtiyya

Order of India and Pakistan. Both orders are intensely focused on the love of God and cultivating love toward everyone. Both orders also welcome disciples of any religion.

TENSE SITUATIONS AND THE SAFETY NET

Netanel Miles-Yepez: *Now that we have talked about the bases and boundary issues, the models, the friendship, and shared experience that support the dialogical process, I think it is a good time to deal with what happens when things get tense. In twenty years, this has to have happened at least a few times.*

Robert Dunbar: Fortunately, it hasn't happened often, but there have been a few occasions.

Donald Postema: What I like about the Snowmass Conference is that we don't have to agree with one another to continue our friendship or to continue the conversation. People often think that to do interreligious dialogue you have to come to some bland, low-level common denominator . . . and never disagree. However, we know one another well enough to really disagree, *fundamentally*, and not be affected negatively in our relationship. I never had to water down my feelings *or* my tradition; in fact, it was demanded of us that we not do that.

Henoch Dov Hoffman: If we become hesitant to dig in and look at problems, to talk about boundaries, then the whole dialogue has a "Pollyanna-ish" feel to it. It just isn't real. But during this last meeting I suggested we talk about war and peace in our traditions, and the discussion really went beyond where we wanted to go as friends.

Ibrahim Gamard: It started when someone jokingly suggested, "You and Howard [Henoch Dov] are friends, why don't you just settle this whole peace in the Middle East question?" Well, we looked at each other and said, "Sure, we'll talk about it." And we did.

But it's a hard issue and tied to a lot of feelings, and as I spelled things out from the Muslim side and the politics that go with it, and when he did the same, it became heated and tense.

Henoch Dov Hoffman: Yes it did; it really had nothing to do with how we felt about one another, but it had a lot to do with how emotionally involved we were with the subject. These things have always weighed very heavily on me, and it came out in that discussion.

Netanel Miles-Yepez: *What was the "safety net" in that situation?*

Ibrahim Gamard: The friendship was a safety net. In fact, I think we felt even more affection for one another after that; we just knew that this wasn't the place from which we wanted to interact; the friendship was more important. We chose not to debate it like that again and, instead, nurtured our personal bond.

Henoch Dov Hoffman: If you are loved and respected, even in disagreement, that creates safety.

Netanel Miles-Yepez: *Does anyone remember another such occasion?*

Atmarupananda: Once, we were discussing Hans Küng's effort to create a "universal ethic" at the Parliament of World Religions in Chicago in 1993 and found ourselves in a heated debate. Küng had written a book about this universal ethic and was trying to get it ratified by the parliament in 1993. But the representative of the Ramakrishna Order (and a few others) refused to sign it, feeling it was too oriented toward the Abrahamic religions, and this caused some bad feelings. Raimundo Panikkar also told us that he was opposed to it for the same reason.

After the parliament, we were discussing that effort, hoping to give Küng some input in his efforts to refine it. But, just as in the parliament, a couple of us had difficulties with statements about human nature being sinful, weak, and dependent on God.

From the Vedanta and the Vajrayana Buddhist viewpoints, human nature is pure—that purity merely being obscured by ignorance. So I said I couldn't agree with a statement phrased like that. I could understand where it was coming from, and that we do sometimes find ourselves weak and fallible, but part of the problem is that we think of ourselves that way. Well, this caused an unexpected uproar and some of the strongest exchanges I can remember at the Snowmass Conference. One person fired back at me, "You make it sound as if you are all born from the Immaculate Conception!" And another said, "Obviously we are sinful; look at the world, read the newspaper!" I understood where they were coming from, but those of us who took this position also felt strongly. In my experience, it was the most unbridgeable moment we came to in the group.

Netanel Miles-Yepez: *Were you able to "hold" that confrontation in the dialogue space?*

Atmarupananda: Sadly, we never really resolved it; it became so heated that it was just dropped; we tabled it. It was one of the few times where we didn't come to some sort of resolution and understanding in the group, saying, "This is where you come from, and this is where we come from; they're different and that's okay." For some reason, the feelings around this issue were very strong.

Sometimes, the tensions and entrenchment can't be dealt with in the formal dialogue. When we have heated exchanges in the Snowmass Conference over misunderstandings or disagreements, we are able to go to that person afterward and straighten out the situation one on one, so that resentment doesn't become a part of the group dynamic. We can talk in a friendly way without anyone else hearing, chitchat and talk about the tension itself and what had caused it in the meeting, and that allows us to remain friends and to continue our dialogue. And this is what had to be done in this situation.

Netanel Miles-Yepez: *So even in a safe dialogue space, obviously there isn't a place in the formal dialogue to get up and walk over to have a personal word with that person to heal the situation?*

Atmarupananda: No, it would interrupt the flow of the dialogue for the others, the work of twelve people for the disagreement of two. So this comes back to the issue of why separate socializing is essential to the dialogue. Some things can be fixed only in private.

CHAPTER FOUR

THE WORK OF DIALOGUE

THE JOYS OF DIALOGUE

Netanel Miles-Yepez: *Earlier Robert mentioned how he was always hoping to learn something new, or to be inspired by the dialogue; what are some of the other joys and attractions of this kind of dialogue?*

Atmarupananda: When I first came into the Snowmass Conference in 1995, people were already talking about ending it, and I was really upset; I had just come and found this wonderful dialogue unlike any other I had ever been a part of, and here they are talking about ending it! I just couldn't believe people would want to give this up, and I still can't.

When I lived in California, I helped to found the Interreligious Council of San Diego. It was an active council and did important work, facing social problems with a united front. But it was not inwardly satisfying for me, because its purpose was not to share on an intimate spiritual level. It was important work; it just didn't have the dialogical dimension I longed for. Later, I attended the Parliament of World Religions in 1993, and there were recognized and famous representatives from all different traditions, an amazing collection of minds ready for dialogue. And it was a good event, and I am glad that I went, but it was nothing compared to the Snowmass Conference. The people here, with the exception of Father Tom, are not famous, and yet the dialogue is exceptional—not to mention the camaraderie and deep friendliness. And this is still the attraction for me: the quality of the people and the quality of the dialogue. Without their level of experience and engagement it wouldn't have held together and wouldn't be as worthwhile.

Sudha Puri: These meetings were always the peak experience of my year. It is a wonderful opportunity to be present with such people—people who have grown to be such close friends. I especially loved the intimate sharing over meals and, oh, the stories we shared about our experiences with great teachers. Funny stories and rich teachings! There is nothing else like it.

Netanel Miles-Yepez: *How about you, Tania; what have you loved most?*

Tania Leontov: There are so many things, but I really loved hearing about other people's inspirational moments; these were always very attractive to me, and still are.

Father George Timko had a very traditional congregation, and very few people he could really share his mystical experience with. It seemed like something had always happened to him through the year, some epiphany, and I always waited expectantly to hear what insight he had had the previous year. He was such a genuine, earthy person, and his insights were always instructive and inspiring.

Netanel Miles-Yepez: *The Reverend Howard Thurman used to say, "Mystical experience isn't something you can explain to people, but it is something you can intoxicate them with."*

Tania Leontov: Yes, and I looked forward to that inspiration. I was also very interested on a very practical level in how people worked with their congregations and students, how they shared insights and urgencies.

Netanel Miles-Yepez: *I have also heard Rabbi Zalman Schachter-Shalomi say, "Nothing inspires us and turns us on to do better on our own side as much as looking across the fence at how other people are doing it."*

Donald Postema: I have found that to be true in my experience of "looking across the fence" at members of the Snowmass Conference. I have experienced what the Quaker Douglas Steere called "Mutual Irradiation." I like to call it "Mutual Illumination." "It is a relationship . . . in which each [religion] is willing to expose itself with great openness to the inward message of the other, as well as to share its own experience, and to trust that whatever is the truth in each experience will irradiate and deepen the experience of the other. . . . It is not likely to leave any of the participants as they were when they started." As we discuss and interact, teachings and practices from another religion shed light on what I believe; I hear things that clarify or challenge my own beliefs and practices. By being willing to be open and to share, to listen and to speak undefensively, my own understanding and *experience* of Christianity has been illumined. I clarified what I believe as I tried to express it to others who do not share my perspective. I found new ways to express my own spirituality. I deepened in my own practice of Christianity and came out of the discussions more committed to my own tradition—from a deeper perspective. So I am grateful for the witness and the "mutual illumination" from the other members.

THE INTERPERSONAL DYNAMICS OF DIALOGUE

Netanel Miles-Yepez: *We have talked a little about the importance of "wisdom holders" and the importance of friendship; but I would like to look a bit closer at the sociogram of these relationships, as Robert put it—not a dry analysis, but just some of your thoughts on why some friendships and mentorships worked?*

Atmarupananda: I suppose a lot of it depended on personality chemistry; I feel close to everyone, but there are some personalities with whom I hit it off and shared ideas with more readily. For instance, Tania's tradition is the closest to mine in terms of the basic philosophical structures and viewpoints, so we often found ourselves allied on a number of issues. Obviously, there are differences, but in many ways we shared a basic viewpoint.

Sudha Puri: Yes, and I always appreciated how Tania could rein things in when theological discussions got too rarified, bringing us back from the stratosphere. She is wonderfully intelligent, and has a talent for this. You need a person to do that in a group.

Tania Leontov: I always respected Father Tom and Gayatri Devi for doing just that; perhaps they were good models for me. Gayatri Devi had a mind like a sword; you saw it only occasionally, but once in a while it would come out, and it would be a total shock for its brilliance!

Ibrahim Gamard: Gayatri Devi also had a deep mystical presence, and I always felt a great kinship with her because she was *bhakti*, a devotee, and I am very devotional. I often felt that we were coming from the same place, one on one, and in group discussions; the focus with her was always on the love of God.

Roger La Borde: She was really a sweetheart, the epitome of devotion; she would never say anything to offend anybody in the group.

Tania Leontov: Gayatri Devi took me under her wing in a certain way, and I really felt mentored by her. I was one of Trungpa Rinpoche's first teachers, but after I got married and went into business I stopped teaching for a long time. At one point, Gayatri Devi invited me out of nowhere to come and teach at her ashram. It was a terrifying experience, I actually shook on stage, but I was so grateful to her—and who knows why she did it.

Every once in a while, simultaneous with a time when I was feeling down, a little box of *prasad* from her shrine or a little gift would come. Once she sent me one of her cashmere meditation shawls and invited me to come back and teach. That was the maternal aspect of the guru. We didn't have a lot of personal conversations, but her quality, her vastness, her compassion was beyond measure and always present.

Thomas Keating: Sudha has really taken on Ma's mantle very well, both in teaching and in running the ashrams on the East Coast and the West. She and I also share a monastic background; she used to be an Anglican nun. And she took care of Ma very well, especially after her terrible automobile accident. So we love her on her own and also for what she was to Ma.

Atmarupananda: If we are talking about a sociogram of dialogue and roles, I have always felt Roger [La Borde] was important in this regard. He is a shaman and has always represented the "non-aligned" position, emphasizing the individual path. I have always liked the outsider, and Roger is ever ready to challenge any viewpoint he feels is insubstantial. I like that; I feel it serves a function in our meetings. And I like him as a person.

Netanel Miles-Yepez: *That's an important point. It may be that Roger is a necessary ingredient in this dialogue, not only as a "holy gadfly," but in terms of the sociogram. His shamanism, which is rooted in personal spirituality, forces him to question certain assumptions that a group of seasoned practitioners from long-established traditions would not. Whether religion is important, whether meditation is important—these issues might not even be brought up without someone like him in the group.*

Atmarupananda: That's very true, I agree one hundred percent; things like authority structures—all of our traditions have some authority structure, and Roger's doesn't. He has teachers he respected and learned from, but no organizational structure or hierarchy, so he questions that when others do not; we may question the form it takes, but rarely the necessity of it. Another thing is the sacred text; he doesn't have one. His is a living text, and so he challenges us. I like that, personally, and I value his input. I have even felt protective of him when others haven't cared for that—not that he needs it!

Roger La Borde: Well . . . what can I say about that? Sometimes it just feels necessary to call them long-winded, boring sermoniz-

ers—to confront people about these things. I am not much interested in quotes from the Bhagavad-Gita, Dogen, the Bible,
Qur'an, or the Talmud. What I am interested in is this, "Why did
you decide to go on the journey you did?" Like with Father Tom,
I wanted to know why, at twenty years old, a graduate of Yale
and Fordham from a very well-off family went into one of the
most austere religious orders in the world. What was he looking
for, and did he find it? That's what I am interested in. So I am
always pushing for that substance—basically, to get to the point
where we can be comfortable being "naked" in front of each
other. That has happened, and it cemented the group. Everyone
began talking about their successes, failures, disappointments,
and joys, and there is absolutely no subject in this group that is
taboo. So I think it has been worthwhile to push the boundaries.

Thomas Keating: Roger carries the pipe of Grandfather Gerald Red
Elk, so he is not entirely without credentials; but he is definitely
"nonaligned," as we have always defined him. He does remarkable work with people in comas, and while he would not call
himself part of the Native American tradition, he is the best
source we have for that tradition. We've tried Native Americans,
but Red Elk left a big footprint. And it is only Roger who seems
to have carried on what Red Elk was doing. He provides a very
valuable perspective. We treasure his presence and are honored
by the fact that he stuck it out with us from the very beginning.

Roger La Borde: For many years, I saw it as my task to keep Gerald's
spirit alive in the group, and at this last meeting I told them that
I felt I had honored my commitment to Gerald. And now that it
was fulfilled, I would declare a position as a shaman, which I was
reluctant to do before. Everyone was always trying to figure me
out. So I was called in the beginning, "a representative of the un-
churched" and "non-aligned," and I agreed; I *am* out of alignment! And I don't think you can ever get me into alignment. The
connection that I have is from a shamanic perspective.
Shamanism at its core is really connected to nothing but one's
personal experience with the Ultimate Mystery. Tom has always

been tremendously supportive of me and respectful of my path. In fact, in the fourth or fifth year he told me that he had overlooked in me the oldest tradition in the world, which is that of no tradition.

Thomas Keating: In this category of "nonaligned" was also our beloved Jim Barnett. We first knew him as **Swami Buddhananda** when he was our Hindu Vedanta representative. And like Swami Atmarupananda, he is extremely articulate and talented and had a lot of psychological know-how and healing gifts. He belonged to the Ramakrishna Order for many years, but decided to leave that path to take a path that was closer to the Earth for him. He was a major contributor while he was with us.

Netanel Miles-Yepez: *Jim mentioned to me that he fondly remembered Father Keating noting, "Here we have Roger, who doesn't believe in any path, and Jim, who believes in them all!"*

Roger La Borde: I had (and have) a wonderful connection with Jim Barnett. It was in our third meeting that he left the order, and we respected his decision. Eventually, he decided to stop coming for a number of reasons, but one was that he didn't feel we needed two representatives of the nonaligned! He and I both believe that there is a world of difference between religion and spirituality; he likes to say, "We are spiritual beings having a human experience."

Robert Dunbar: I think common experience also counts for a lot in the sociogram. Swami Atmarupananda and I had so much in common in our backgrounds, both growing up Presbyterians in South Carolina; I even knew some of his family. We also had Vedanta in common and had even met before in San Diego in the Vedanta center there. Likewise, Don Postema and I shared a common experience of the Reformed Church—me once working in a Dutch Reformed church, and he being Christian Reformed. We had mutual acquaintances and drew on parallel knowledge of Christian Calvinist sources.

Donald Postema: Yes, the friendship Robert and I forged was natural and has been an inspiration to me. Since he came from a similar tradition, he was one person who could understand where I was coming from, even if he didn't agree with me.

Similarly, Ibrahim and I met on the plane flying to our first meeting at Mount Holyoke. He had never met a Calvinist before, so he looked up "Calvinism" in an encyclopedia and later said to me, "We have a lot of similar beliefs." This both endeared Ibrahim to me and sometimes frustrated me. Some things he'd say in discussions were so close to what I was trying to shed from my tradition that I'd get irritated with *him*. He always took that with good humor.

Robert Dunbar: Each year more trust developed in the group, and we became friends who really looked forward to seeing one another.

Edward Bastian: There were a number of members with whom I shared a scholarly background, and it was a real pleasure to share those insights with them. It is rare to have so many scholars with deep spiritual experience in one place together; I found it extremely stimulating.

Netanel Miles-Yepez: *Sometimes, it seems to me, it is easier to find a peer group outside of your own tradition.*

Sudha Puri: That's an interesting point. I actually don't share on this level with many people in my own tradition—except perhaps Swami Atmarupananda, who is also in the group. So, yes, I think there may be something to that.

Netanel Miles-Yepez: *I think the dialogue is often different with members of your own tradition, primarily because you usually end up falling into "insider talk," and "insider politics." But with a peer group made up mostly of people from different traditions, the common language usually has to do with deep structures of practice.*

Donald Postema: Yes, as religious professionals, we can speak about our successes, failures, aspirations, and frustrations and be understood. There are no hidden agendas or power struggles with each other, so we can just speak about what we value in our traditions and share difficulties we have with them and receive empathetic counsel and encouragement. I value this very much.

Sudha Puri: And it really wouldn't work unless you could meet in those deep places, around the inner life.

THEOLOGY IN DIALOGUE

Netanel Miles-Yepez: *When Ed mentioned "scholarship," I was reminded of theology; working so diligently on the "Points of Agreement" must have taken you often enough into the tricky territory of theology. Did any of you find the dialogue of theology helpful?*

Tania Leontov: I personally feel I have learned an enormous amount by discussing the theology of various traditions, and a number of my assumptions have been overturned by what I have learned. The truth is, you need some of it at the beginning to see that there are other views, and when you are working with true practitioners who have integrated this with their own personal experience, it can be an interesting discussion, absent of dogma. So I would say I found value in the dialogue of theology, generally, but not when it predominated.

Netanel Miles-Yepez: *Can you give me an example of a situation where theology predominated?*

Tania Leontov: Occasionally, people from different sects or lineages of the same tradition can fall into a private dialogue in the midst of the group about points of divergence within their own tradition, and if it goes on too long it tends to put everyone else on the outside and become quite boring. Father Tom was always good about putting a stop to this and undercutting this kind of insular dialogue.

Sudha Puri: It was always interesting to watch how different people reacted to theological discussions. In particular, I remember how Grandfather Red Elk's eyes would glaze over and start to close whenever we got mired in theology; he had little interest in abstractions. But as soon as the discussion returned to real experience, he would become energized again. It was like there was an energy switch continually turning on and off for him.

There were definitely times when it was necessary to get into the details of theology, but it was always best when we were talking straight from the marrow of our experience. If this happened to differ from our tradition's theology, we weren't afraid to say so.

Roger La Borde: Occasionally, it was interesting to hear the finer points of theology, but generally I wasn't interested in that. It was a nice aside and curiosity for my memory bank, but not very important to me.

Netanel Miles-Yepez: *Obviously, there are both strengths and weaknesses to the dialogue of theology, and many of the weaknesses seem to have something to do with whether or not the theology is based in personal experience. Would someone mind saying a little more about this?*

Donald Postema: When I came to my first meeting, in Mount Holyoke, I came loaded with a great desire to talk about my *ideas* about God; but to my shock I found almost everyone one else talking about their *experience* of the Divine! I was overwhelmed by that, and really had to rethink what was going on and what I was doing there. I think theology and ideas are important, but they have to be connected with experience. "What does this mean for my spiritual life?" That was the purity Father Thomas was constantly bringing to the group and the purity that changed my whole approach to dialogue.

It has been an honor, as a Protestant Christian, to be part of this group that is concerned about the spiritual aspects of our traditions. I am deeply committed to my roots in Calvinism, and we too have a tradition of piety. John Calvin said that the spiritual life is like "a three-legged stool": it is based on the "knowledge of God," the "service of God," and the "experience of God." Now, the tradition has always been strong on and emphasized the first two "legs," but has not been as comfortable with the third. I was doing the "knowledge" part when I started in the group, but I have always been looking for the "experience." That was the reason I wrote my book *Space for God*; I was looking for more of the experience of God in my own tradition. The "experience" of others in this group inspired me to look harder for it in my own tradition.

Atmarupananda: Too often, theology is born of a situation in which an intellectual (not necessarily a spiritually experienced one) has read scripture and then considered the rational implications for the tradition. But from a Vedantic standpoint—at least ideally— theology is only an explanation for experience. When we just intellectualize without understanding the inner experience it can obscure rather than clarify. Certainly in Hindu philosophy you will find plenty of fine distinctions that can get divorced from experience, but it is understood ideally that to be a true theologian or philosopher one has to be a person of deep experience. First comes experience and, only then, the explanation in rational terms, the means by which it can be conveyed from one mind to another.

This is even more important in philosophy, because it speaks more in terms of principles that any educated mind can understand, whether Chinese, Indian, African or American. Theology, however, exists within a context that is cultural and mythological (a symbolic world of experience and dialogue). Nevertheless, these rational explanations become problematic when we use them to defend ourselves from others, to keep from listening to another who is saying something that our theology doesn't recognize. It can be used as a means of expression or as a means of defense and aggression. But as an explanation for the context of our experience, it is useful. In dialogue, it is good to stick to experience.

Henoch Dov Hoffman: The dialogue of theology is useful, but better is just a good open discussion of issues.

THE DISCIPLINE OF DIALOGUE

Netanel Miles-Yepez: *This, I think, brings us to the "work," or "discipline," of dialogue. Beyond everything else, something is supposed to come of this talk, and it takes some skill and effort. What is that skill, and what is that effort?*

Henoch Dov Hoffman: One skill has to do with what I call "dialogics." It is a fusion of ideas that is dependent on marking the differences as essential. In Hegelian dialectics, the thesis and antithesis are lost in the synthesis, but in dialogics, they are preserved; this is what I think we have in the Snowmass Conference.

This has been a feature of Jewish internal dialogue through the ages—that it is absolutely vital to the integrity of human beings and God, man and woman, to have the integrity of their boundaries preserved, and without that there is no effective or Godly fusion. So, in dialogics, as I have formulated it, the integrity of each party is absolutely necessary, and I have just transposed that over to the religious dialogue. There may be fusion, but there is no synthesis. For me, this is part of the knowledge of dialogue, and applying it is one of the skills of dialogue.

Netanel Miles-Yepez: *How about effort? If we look at the dialogue as an environment where spiritual growth may occur, can anyone discern any internal development in themselves as a result of dialogue? Father Keating?*

Thomas Keating: Oh, sure! I certainly have a greater respect and understanding of the other world religions; a greater openness and admiration for their methods and teachings; a greater sense of communion with the people who are practicing; and a sense of the oneness of human nature. It has greatly expanded my own worldview and understanding of the Christian religion and, if anything, has deepened and enriched it. I find a lot of insight in dialogue that helps me to better understand the Christian scriptures or to explain them from a more contemplative perspective. In every way I feel that it is enriching and valuable.

Netanel Miles-Yepez: *And what effort was necessary to bring that about?*

Thomas Keating: In the beginning, given the narrowness of my perspective, it required a strict discipline of trying to bracket my own ideas and to be open to seeing them from a different perspective. True dialogue is an ascetical discipline. It really is quite searching at times and challenging to one's presuppositions. Sometimes you are left trying to figure out how it all fits together: How can I explain this from a Christian perspective? How do I recognize and uphold the truth of this non-Christian presentation in the Christian worldview? Sometimes the two seem opposed, and it requires some soul-searching reflection and a willingness to change.

Ultimately, I find it liberates one from aspects of one's tradition that are cultural and not of the essence of the teaching. Usually these have become so intermingled with the essence over the centuries that you cannot discern the difference without being challenged to look at the whole thing from a an objective perspective. And that isn't so easy to do. It requires time, energy, and courage, but I have felt impelled to do that in my dialoguing, especially as part of the Snowmass Conference.

Donald Postema: When you are a part of a group like this, you have hard questions asked about your core beliefs, some verbal and others born just from a confrontation with something different and challenging. But all of these questions helped me to articulate better answers, both for others and for me; it deepened my own journey. The different points of view were really challenging, especially in the beginning. I always had to go home to process and rethink things. This wasn't easy. I think it took me a year to process what had happened to me in my first meeting.

Netanel Miles-Yepez: *So real dialogue requires a certain spiritual askesis?*

Thomas Keating: That's right. Often the question is: How in the world am I going to harmonize this with what I have always taught and believed? And the answer is: You have to go slowly and be willing to unwrap your prepackaged values. It's a demanding discipline. Those who don't have a good grasp of their own traditions (and I am afraid that is the majority of religious people) should go into dialogue advisedly. Often, when these people get into the deeper aspects of dialogue, they don't quite know how to handle it. You need to have a point of departure for discussion and evaluation and some sense of what is nonessential in one's own belief system.

It is a process of unfolding over a long period of time, an openness to the subtle changes that take place in oneself, an open vulnerability to the wisdom of other teachings. Now I find this very enriching and enjoy it. Hearing the explanations today, they no longer seem contradictory to anything in the Christian mystical tradition. But it wasn't always that way; so that is some sort of progression, though perhaps others will think it a *regression*.

Donald Postema: Reflection during and after our meetings has produced some deep insights in me, and also some profound, often disturbing questions. My view of the vastness and creativity of the Divine has definitely been expanded by my own experience of holy diversity. That was a real challenge for me and forced me to ask: Did God actually intend and create us to be diverse, not only as cultures and peoples but also as religions? And does God listen to the prayers and meditations of other people of faith? If not, then why not? What kind of God wouldn't listen? But if God does listen and accept, what becomes of the exclusivist view of

God lurking in my soul? I believe Jesus is a unique revelation of the Divine intention for the world, but does this uniqueness of Jesus mean that the story of Jesus is the only story of the Divine presence on Earth? These were not easy questions for me to face, but that is just what honest dialogue forced me to do.

Jesus was not a Christian but a Jew, and it helped me to understand him better when I understood the Jewish tradition better. After meetings, I have often gone on to study more about the various religions represented in the Snowmass Conference, and I have been personally challenged to find what comes from the heart of my tradition that can reach the heart of persons from other traditions.

Henoch Dov Hoffman: In most discussions or debates, people are ego-identified with their positions, and everything gets taken personally. But the discipline of dialogue requires that we try to separate the ego from the position. And this process is also part of the dialogue. This is the idea of learning from the shadow, the dark places in our psychological life. The darkness is rich in potential opportunities for spiritual growth. I believe the safety zone of dialogue is increased every time we get onto these touchy topics and express a greater range of feelings.

Netanel Miles-Yepez: *This brings up an interesting point. We rarely come to dialogue with a clean slate; we have these assumptions and experiences, not all of them positive, and we, often unwittingly, bring them to the dialogue environment. In other words, they are in "shadow" for us, influencing what we say and how we react without us being fully conscious of them. Does anyone else think this is an important consideration in dialogue?*

Tania Leontov: Though I was born Jewish, I was not a religious person growing up; religions just weren't particularly interesting to me. Even after I became a Buddhist, I had a very primitive notion of Judaism and Christianity; I really had no idea what either was about.

When I was twelve, I came to the conclusion that there was no such thing as Gŏd. So theism for me was always a marvel; I couldn't believe that others would allow themselves to be so deluded; I questioned what it was in people that made them need that. It seemed to me that they were abdicating responsibility in a way. And I am sure I brought this to my earliest attempts at dialogue. But as I began to have more exposure to the subtle understandings of God through the lens of my Buddhism, I really felt that the difference was so subtle that in most ways it didn't matter any more that there was a difference. It certainly was different in how people spoke about things, but the mystical understandings seemed very close and in harmony.

When I first met Father Keating, it had never occurred to me as possible that a Christian could attain enlightenment. That was implicit in the conclusion I drew in childhood. I thought of enlightenment only in terms of Buddhism. But with Father Keating I felt that I was looking at the nature of enlightenment as it unfolds in another path. I mean Father Tom evolved over a period of time, but I always felt that he was a vast soul. To see his boundless compassion and wisdom turned me around.

Netanel Miles-Yepez: *Dialogue gave you the opportunity to evolve a twelve-year-old's assumption that had been in stasis for a while.*

Atmarupananda: Another issue is simple ignorance. Until I began to engage in dialogue, I was probably more ignorant of Jewish mysticism than any other of the traditions. I knew of its existence, but that was about it. So it was a real revelation to me to hear Rabbi Miles Krassen, Rami Shapiro, and Howard [Henoch Dov] Hoffman talk about a tradition I recognized, albeit in analogous Jewish terms. When Rabbi Hoffman speaks from the Jewish perspective, I almost always feel, well, I see it a little differently, but I don't have a single problem with it, even in the corners. So that is the illumining of ignorance that can come from dialogue.

Roger La Borde: The fact that we have these hidden "slivers" from our past is a good reason to try to cultivate the right attitude before dialogue. I go into it the same way I go into a healing situation; I have no idea what is going happen, so I try to be a blank slate, and I wait. Even though I know everyone, I try to go into it fresh, waiting for inspiration.

Netanel Miles-Yepez: *I want to turn the dial a bit now and ask about resistance in dialogue. Often there is a resistance point in the dialogue, a point at which some feel that they might be betraying their own tradition if they go any further. How do you mediate that for them in a group?*

Thomas Keating: It is understood in our group that nobody has to participate in anything that is uncomfortable. If it works for you, fine; if it doesn't, that's fine, too. But we also want them to be able to express their discomfort or contrary belief without worrying too much about stepping on somebody else's toes. That's what dialogue is all about. We don't want to pretend that we agree when we don't. So that is one of the benefits of discussing what we don't agree about, and it helps to purify our own integrity in upholding what we feel our faith requires of us. Sometimes the differences are more enriching than what we agree about.

On the other hand, it may well be that we exaggerate how much is required of us, so you ask some really deep questions: What is the most essential aspect? What is the ultimate experience? Is it the same in all religions? Since we translate any deep experience, it ceases to be what it was and now it is interpreted through our own belief systems and can only approximate the original insight. So with all of the fun we have to add this element of rigor. Rigor is also necessary for less exalted reasons. Sometimes it is a little tiresome to listen to long explanations. But if you make up your mind that this is the job of the present moment, after a lull in the conversation, sometimes it takes off. I think a higher intelligence sometimes gets into the act, and a discussion becomes extremely profound and enriching.

Robert Dunbar: I think it is a good sign that the meetings get boring occasionally, because it means that we are no longer "exotic" to one another.

Netanel Miles-Yepez: *Have you found any way of working with a fundamentalist position in dialogue? Father Keating?*

Thomas Keating: [chuckles] Not so far! They are not very willing to speak to me; they think I am a disaster. They have a very literal interpretation of scripture, which can be very frustrating and painful, because it doesn't do justice to the text or to its transformative potential. There is a meaning behind the text and a mystery to which it can only point.

Donald Postema: There are folks in my tradition who wonder why I'm part of this group, if my purpose is not "witnessing" to or proselytizing the other members. I understand their concern. My answer is that I try to be the best Calvinist I can be so that I have something unique to offer the members from other religions. Also, I believe there is another stance to take toward other people of faith—namely, hospitality. Hospitality toward strangers is a biblical virtue, whether the stranger is a person or an *idea*. I believe that hospitality is not only an ethical virtue but an epistemological virtue as well. So I approach interreligious conversation as a person who is committed, yet open. I believe there is a witness of listening as well as a witness of talking.

Netanel Miles-Yepez: *Swami Prabhavananda, one of the great teachers in the Ramakrishna lineage, and Jim Barnett's teacher, said, "We didn't come to Hinduize the world; we came to spiritualize it!"*

THE LESSONS OF DIALOGUE

Netanel Miles-Yepez: *Over time you get a sense of what makes for a good dialogue. Often it is attitudes, or environment, and these begin to coalesce into a whole. What are some of the lessons you have learned about what makes a good dialogue work?*

Atmarupananda: The first thing is well enough known to be a cliché, but the problem with clichés is that we forget the point of them, remembering only the words. Nevertheless, for me, the ability to listen and hear what the other person is actually saying is essential. Now, this kind of listening doesn't come from mere politeness, and this is a mistake that is often made; true listening can happen only if you sincerely believe that the other person is really trying to say something important. This may sound obvious, but it is not obvious at all. People are usually so focused on what *they* have to say that they don't really listen, and then they don't understand and think the fault is with the person they weren't listening to. So we must have the willingness *and* the ability to listen—two different things. Some people are willing, but don't know how. You must come with the conviction that the others have something to say that is valuable. You may not agree with it, but they wouldn't be speaking unless it was meaningful to them. So it becomes your task to find out *why* it is meaningful to them: What are they trying to say, and in what context are they saying it? All of these things have to fit together, and this is extremely important to a successful dialogue.

Vivekananda teaches that anybody who has thought deeply about life, human experience and the cosmos has something to say that is important. One may not agree with that person, but it is important to listen. For instance, in the 1950s to listen to anything that came from Karl Marx would be difficult for an American because of the rampant hatred for Communism that was current then. And though as a religious person I am obviously not a Marxist, I believe Marx had something important to say. He had thought a great deal about the human condition, and though I may disagree with his solutions his analysis of human problems has a lot to say to us. Likewise, I am not a Freudian, but the truth is Sigmund Freud looked deeply into the human mind and had important things to say. It is not enough to dismiss him, saying, "He was all about sexual repression." Freud wasn't a Freudian and Marx wasn't a Communist; they were just trying to figure things out, and because of that they learned important lessons.

So there may be ways of looking at religion that are not natural to me personally, but I should not close them out either, saying, "That poor misguided person. Thank God I know better."

You may not agree with everyone, but for dialogue to be rich, you should have the conviction that "others have unique perceptions of reality, and if I really listen, I am going to learn something." Of course, we must be realistic also; in any gathering of people, someone comes more to talk than to listen, and that is destructive to dialogue.

Tania Leontov: You have to establish a basis of friendship, or you don't get to genuine dialogue. You have to be courageous, because sometimes what you are going to say will not suit everyone. But you have to remain true to your experience and say it; be thoughtful and precise in explaining what it is about, but say it with courage. You also have to be willing to say "I don't understand" or "This is a question for me. Can we talk about it further?" You are there as a contributor and you have to have the dignity and the courage of that role—to be both vulnerable and honest.

Sudha Puri: One has to have trust, honesty and humility. The attitude of the learner, as opposed to the pontificator, is essential. If you are just starting in a dialogue group, you also should have the humility to have reasonable expectations about what can be done in the amount of time given. Go slowly, step by step. This group evolved step by step.

A certain amount of continuity in the group is also necessary. Nor can you have someone who is constantly pulling the group down, or attacking others. There is no room for that in the environment of sacred dialogue.

Atmarupananda: You also need differences of opinion, different viewpoints. If it were just me and Tania or Howard, we may just begin to meet to have fun together, but probably wouldn't have much dialogue after a while; it would just become a back-patting session—"you're just like me"—the death of the real dialogue.

Netanel Miles-Yepez: *Counterpoint.*

Henoch Dov Hoffman: I think you have to let people know what your sensibilities are, what your boundaries are, but also express to them your willingness to be open and to work on the difficult issues. I think my propensity for open discussion still grates on some people—my desire to explore the dark undersides of things—but it is really necessary. You don't bring people together to just state their positions and call that ecumenism. You can read a book for that information. Unless you build the trust between those individuals, you are not really going anywhere. Dialogue is about developing that trust.

Donald Postema: Often when people talk about dialogue, the word "tolerance" is tossed around as if it is at the heart of dialogue. Tolerance is a prerequisite, a beginning, but it is too shallow a concept for real dialogue. It's no fun to simply be tolerated. What is needed for real dialogue are respect, hospitality, openness, vulnerability and appreciation. Some folks fear they may lose their moorings and be set adrift with such intense interaction. And that may be true, and thus it takes some maturity in one's faith and a solid grounding in one's tradition to enter this kind of dialogue. It also means that I have a responsibility to speak my part of truth as a gift to others in my tradition and to the world religious community as well as to listen with respect to others.

THE FRUIT OF DIALOGUE

Netanel Miles-Yepez: *The philosopher Ken Wilber has a criticism of what often happens in dialogue today—that it is often "flat." You have a circle, and many viewpoints are expressed, as Reb Henoch Dov mentioned, but that is all that happens; it is just talk, and remains flat; it doesn't have a spiral dynamic to it, it doesn't ascend to any purpose. If dialogue isn't just "talk," what has been the fruit of this dialogue?*

Sudha Puri: There is no nourishment in those horizontal dialogues, and here we have definitely been nourished. I am always encouraged to work even harder on my inner life by association with these people; I am enriched by what people share, and their traditions illuminate my own tradition. The utter sincerity of the group is peerless. I have never experienced anything else like it in my life. When you do real spiritual work, the effect ripples out over the whole universe, whether people know it or not. Things change when deep inner work is done by a group like this. My own congregation has certainly been enriched by it, and I think the "Points of Agreement" are the black-and-white "fruit" of this kind of dialogue.

At our last meeting, a number of people mentioned what we have all known for years: we are all out there for one another, and we can tune in and support one another in prayer at any time, every day, and this is a tremendous comfort and help.

Atmarupananda: I agree with Wilber's criticism. This is often what happens; dialogue is reduced to a "flatland" of two-dimensional views put out for everyone to see, but no one is changed by any of it. For me, there is a deep learning that takes place; the intellectual encounter with another tradition through books is replaced by a positive confrontation with reality, with another person who actually believes this and believes it deeply. You can read a book about comparative religions and see them two-dimensionally, and even have a two-dimensional dialogue, but encountering another person of spiritual depth affects one personally. When you hear someone speak with depth and conviction, the experience is transforming.

I have also seen people who have entered dialogue with relatively narrow theological frameworks, and who, in time, expand in extraordinary ways through this encounter. But even beyond this, when the dialogue is good we share an experience of flowing with a higher intelligence; our individual understanding seems uplifted into a collective sharing with something higher. This is how Father Tom expressed it at our last meeting. In a sense, this is the most important aspect of dialogue. It doesn't always happen, but when it does, there is nothing like it. When we are immersed in the wisdom of that collective sharing, a higher understanding descends on all of the individuals.

Ibrahim Gamard: Prayer has power, and there is an effect from our sitting in silence together, from our meeting together; we are a part of something that is a wish for humanity, expressing a wish that all traditions can live in peace together.

Roger La Borde: Since 1992, I have been in all kinds of healing situations where I have helped families with a loved one in a coma, and they have been Hindus, Muslims, Jews, and Christians. Snowmass has given me a greater knowledge and understanding of different religious paths. So now, when I enter into a family situation like this, I can talk to them about their loved one, using terminology that they would understand from their own spiritual path. It has been a really wonderful resource for me to be able to use that information and knowledge to help others.

Anytime a person in a place of influence has changed in the sense of becoming more awake or aware to larger realms, then it is definitely felt, seen, or translated in some way to other people they are involved with.

Tania Leontov: I am now the director of two small nonprofits: the Buddhist Coalition for Bodhisattva Activity, which nurtures partnerships between Buddhist sanghas and human service agencies' outreach work; and the other is Restoring the Soul: Faith and Community Partnerships, which is interfaith outreach. I feel it has really confirmed a passion in me for collaboration, and also in the crucial role spiritual life has to play in human endeavor. In a very basic way, I just feel more at home in the world; people don't feel strange just because they believe different things. I feel I can approach many traditions easily, because I have had an intimate experience of them.

This conference will be difficult to replicate. These people are special. It is unusual to find so many wisdom holders in one place in such an atmosphere of friendship. But I am hoping that this example will inspire other groups to really stretch themselves.

Ibrahim Gamard: Father Thomas always wanted each of us to have our own private dialogue group in our own town or city where we lived. And some members have done that. There was also talk of connecting more formally with other interfaith groups. For this reason, we sent Reverend Don Postema as our representative to South Africa to the Parliament of World Religions.

Donald Postema: I have gone twice to Parliament of World Religions as a representative of the Snowmass Conference—once in 1993 and another time in 1999. It is a fascinating experience to see all of these religions, to witness their rituals, to see firsthand the dazzling diversity of spiritual experience that is available . . . 7,000 people! All of those people, and I was the only Christian Reformed person there; it was humbling. It is not an intimate experience, nor fostering of friendship the way Snowmass is, but it was somehow uplifting and inspiring to hear that profound cacophony of prayers and benedictions over eight days.

I remember at the 1993 Parliament of World Religions, Robert Muller, a former Deputy Secretary General of the United Nations, gave us this passionate challenge: "Put an end to your feuds. We are spiritually diminished because religions cannot come to terms with each other!"

My experiences of interreligious dialogue have influenced me profoundly, and I have dedicated the rest of my life to reconciliation, peace, and hospitality. I have been deeply influenced by the example of the Ecumenical Community of Taizé, France, which was founded by a Swiss Reformed pastor. From them I learned that reconciliation does not mean the victory of some and the humiliation of others. Reconciliation begins with the grateful discovery of the gifts of God in differing traditions. I believe such reconciliation can be ferment for peace and that, for the sake of peace in the world, it is absolutely necessary to begin with peace among religions. The quest for a spirituality of reconciliation is something on which the credibility of our traditions stands or falls; we all need to live according to the best insights of our religions.

Thomas Keating: Yes, and Don Postema has started his own group; I continue to ask others to share this experience. Ed Bastian's Spiritual Paths Foundation is an offshoot of this work, holding interfaith meetings in different places and often including members of this group—myself, Rami Shapiro, and Swami Atmarupananda.

Donald Postema: Inspired by my experience with the Snowmass Conference, I along with other colleagues have helped initiate various interfaith conversations in Ann Arbor, Michigan. These at last evolved into the Interfaith Roundtable of Washtenaw County, which has been meeting once a month for ten years. The group includes leaders from Catholic, Protestant, Episcopal, Jewish, Muslim, Mormon, Church of Scientology, Bahai, and many other religious traditions. It is self-sustaining and very active. Like Snowmass, we discuss some topic at each meeting—even using the Snowmass "Points of Agreement." The various religions in our community now have a human face as people have gradually become friends. We have even sponsored retreats for young people and inspired a spin-off group for lay people.

Edward Bastian: My experience of sharing in the Snowmass Conference was really a breakthrough for me and catalyzed me to move forward in creating the Spiritual Paths Foundation and its interspiritual seminars. What I discovered was that people who shared a contemplative background could sit together in deep meditation and share a common experience. It was not that religions were all the same; they're not. But something in the human spiritual consciousness was shared by people of all traditions. This came home to me so powerfully in the first Snowmass Conference I attended that I began to think: If I could bring together great teachers, following the example of the Snowmass Conference, to meditate together before doing a public program, the shared feeling would be palpable and would have an impact on the program. These same people could lead the people attending the seminar in the exploration of their own contemplative depths and help them to have their own shared experience.

This then would become the true basis of interreligious understanding and peace—not just the words, the tolerance and the commonalities; but also the common experience of sharing at depth. Once people share at this level, they can no longer treat each other inhumanely on the basis of difference in religion.

Sudha Puri: We have always hoped that the effect of Snowmass would radiate out like this. On the Internet, I have even found out about an interreligious group in Uzbekistan inspired directly by the Snowmass Conference.

Netanel Miles-Yepez: *Perhaps it was good that nothing was recorded until now.*

Thomas Keating: Yes, there is an accumulated and embodied wisdom in this group now; it was more important that it be embodied than recorded.

Netanel Miles-Yepez: *Father Keating, as "convener" I'll give you the last word. What do you feel is the primary purpose and contribution of dialogue today?*

Thomas Keating: There is a mutual enrichment and sharing in deep dialogue that gradually dissolves suspicion and allows the religions to work together in the world. On the other hand, I also think that basic understanding, friendship and respect are contributions we can make to the invisible spiritual world of humanity through our dialogue, and I believe that right disposition affects everybody, whether they can see it or not.

FRAGMENTS FROM THE SNOWMASS
CONFERENCE PAST AND PRESENT

Though no session of the Snowmass Conference was ever recorded on tape or digital media, various records of the conferences still remain, including handwritten notes and records of thoughts on specific subjects from the members. We have edited some of these together for this book, to give the reader some idea of the actual flavor of the dialogues, and to preserve some of the wisdom we have collected in twenty years of good conversation. The participants in these dialogues included:

- **Swami Atmarupananda** (Member of the Snowmass Conference, 1995–2004)
- **Dr. Edward W. Bastian** (Member of the Snowmass Conference, 1999–2004)
- **Swami Buddhananda/James Barnett** (Member of the Snowmass Conference, 1984–1998)
- **Ane Pema Chödrön** (Member of the Snowmass Conference, 1984–1991)
- **Reverend Robert B. Dunbar** (Member of the Snowmass Conference, 1987–2004)
- **Dr. Ibrahim Gamard** (Member of the Snowmass Conference, 1988–2004)
- **Srimata Gayatri Devi** (Member of the Snowmass Conference, 1984–1990)
- **Bernard Tetsugen Glassman Sensei** (Member of the Snowmass Conference, 1984)
- **Rabbi Henoch Dov Hoffman** (Member of the Snowmass Conference, 1995–2004)
- **Father Thomas Hopko** (Member of the Snowmass Conference, 1984)

- **Imam Bilal Hyde** (Member of the Snowmass Conference, 1984–1985)
- **Father Thomas Keating** (Convener/ Member of the Snowmass Conference, 1984–2004)
- **Roger La Borde** (Member of the Snowmass Conference, 1985–2004)
- **Tania Leontov** (Member of the Snowmass Conference, 1984–2004)
- **Reverend Donald H. Postema** (Member of the Snowmass Conference, 1988–2004)
- **Grandfather Gerald Red Elk** (Member of the Snowmass Conference, 1984–1985)
- **Rabbi Rami Shapiro** (Member of the Snowmass Conference, 1984–1985)
- **Srimata Sudha Puri** (Member of the Snowmass Conference, 1985–2004)
- **Father George Timko** (Member of the Snowmass Conference, 1985–1999)

CHAPTER FIVE

THE BEGINNING:
EXCERPTS FROM SNOWMASS I

ST. BENEDICT'S MONASTERY, 1984

These fragments were reconstructed from the handwritten notes of Srimata Sudha Puri, taken at St. Benedict's Monastery, Snowmass, Colorado, on October 21–24, 1984.

THE GATES OF UNITY

The following statements are a collection of quotes from the first Snowmass Conference on the essential unity of spiritual paths. (N. M-Y.)

Father Thomas Keating: There are thousands of religions in the world, all of them different, and none of them can convey through words what is Beyond. But . . . perhaps . . . by discussing our personal experiences of that Beyond, we can come up with a common vocabulary for the human experience of approaching the Ultimate. And with that common vocabulary, perhaps we can achieve a measure of unity that will spread just a little peace in the world.

Bernard Glassman Sensei: The primary practice of Zen is meditation (*zazen*), and meditation is for everyone. In our community, the meditation hall is for whoever would practice meditation, whatever their particular tradition. However, that doesn't mean that the hall is homogeneous; though imageless and silent, it still has some of the trappings of our tradition, for in taking these away, we might also be taking away some of the strength of our tradition. Nevertheless, it is a place where practitioners of different paths can deepen their own practice. For I believe that one's own tradition becomes more powerful and deeper through intercourse with other traditions.

But neither have we intermixed the traditions in our community. I am a traditionalist in this regard. The real place of contact is the imageless, wordless meditation hall; *zazen* is the elimination of subject and object. Clergy in our community are ordained in their own traditions, in addition to receiving our senior training; so one might be a rabbi, for instance, *and* a practitioner of Zen. There are no mixed services.

Regular meditation is the core of our community, coupled with study and work. Zen is a synonym for the word *life*. The essence of Zen (which all the koans are getting at) is the *Now*. Zen is the *Is*, and we celebrate the *Is* in all the "isms," the absolute unknowing in all that is relative. We believe in what offends least and opens gates most.

Father Thomas Keating: On his deathbed, Pope John XXIII said, "We should emphasize what unites rather than what divides."

Srimata Gayatri Devi: In California, Swami Paramananda built the Viswamandir, the Temple of the Universal Spirit, whose stained-glass windows depict places of worship from all the major faiths. We human beings receive the light through various "windows." Our religions are the reflections of the sunlight. On our altar it is written, "Truth is One. Men follow it differently through many paths." We respect all religions; we give reverence to all great teachers of the world. Swami Paramananda was the spiritual disciple of Sri Ramakrishna. His teacher would not allow anyone to speak against any religion, or insist that ours is the right one. All one can say is, "This is my religion, and this is right for me."

Imam Bilal Hyde: The flower of Absolute Reality is the Rose. Each tradition is a door into the rose garden. To every nation, God has given a messenger and a Message. The messengers are many; the Message is one—unity. There is no difference between any of the prophets. As we gravitate toward the center, the paths converge. Separation is the disease from which we all suffer—separation from the Beloved. The perfume of the Rose is the fire of Love.

Ane Pema Chödrön: The purpose of life is to go beyond limitations. The point is *not* to depend on a perfect belief system, but to move beyond dogmatic limitations, to avoid limiting the experience of Reality. We use tradition as a way of assisting us to connect with Wisdom, but the pitfall is that we become limited by our vehicle, by the tradition itself! Contemplatives share the same ground of experience, and use their particular vehicles to go beyond a limited perspective.

Bernard Glassman Sensei: The idols on the altar are Buddhas; the Buddhas in your head are idols!

EAST AND WEST ON THE PATH

In chapter two, Father Keating noted that the first session of the Snowmass Conference was always given to getting acquainted with one another through the sharing of spiritual journeys. The words of Srimata Gayatri Devi, given here, were part of her introduction and sharing of her own spiritual journey with the group in the first session. (N. M-Y.)

Srimata Gayatri Devi: I am an Indian, born there and nurtured there in every way until I was nineteen. India endowed me with a spiritual heritage, but I wanted to come to the West. I came to the West to fulfill my own destiny. Innately, there was a conviction, an awareness that for me, there is no East and West, just one world.

When I was twelve years old, I am told, I declared to my grandma (actually my father's aunt), "*Thakurma*, I will be a *brahmacharini*, I will be a celibate." I suppose the experience of meeting my parents' guru, Suranath Brahmachari Baba, was still fresh. He passed on when I was seven, but the softness of his voice was unforgettable. Father told us that when Suranath Brahmachari Baba met his guru, a Himalayan *sadhu* who settled in the valley and lived to be 121, he was directed to live at home between two fires (his two wives) and to practice *brahmacharya*, "celibacy." I remember going to his ashram as a child. I was most impressed with the coolness. India is hot, but the floors there were so cool, and Brahmachari Baba was radiantly beautiful.

In India at that time men and women were kept apart. Women in my day were completely secluded. We went to school in a carriage, and our mother never went out, even though we lived in the city. That was the destiny of a married woman. So when I became of marriageable age, I told my parents that I would not marry. But my father told me, "In our society, a woman has no status unless she is married. Wifehood and motherhood develop a woman." He didn't feel that a single woman developed. Women in India were worshipped as the Divine Mother in speech only!

At about that time, Gandhiji was coming to our city, Dacca, where the Muslim culture was powerful and women were in *purdah*, wearing the veil, and there was to be a mass men's meeting. I was rebellious, and I said to my lawyer father, "Hasn't Gandhiji anything to say to women?" So a meeting for women was set up in the Bar Library. Gandhiji asked all of us to help. He knew there would be many arrests. He said that all our young people would spend time in prison and later would be very respected for having done so. We were invited to join. Father was with Gandhiji in every way except regarding school. We were under British rule for 300 years, and our schools were British. Gandhiji's movement would require boycotting those schools. My brother and his friends were heatedly discussing these issues, and their feeling was "down with the British." My father overheard their words and said to them, "How is it that we are millions in India and a handful of islanders can keep us under their control? Have you ever thought that they might have a touch of greatness?" But I was a rebel. Gandhiji said, "Spin wool and don't wear machine-made saris." I wove and wore "homespun." I wanted so badly to be a Gandhi follower. Yet I trusted my parents, and they made me believe that it was the Lord's will and their guru's direction that I should be given in marriage. Those three years were not the happiest; it was imposed upon me. But it was no doubt Divine will, and I must have had something to learn. At the end of three years, widowhood came—an undesirable state for a woman in India, for no remarriage is possible, and the whole situation was very upsetting to my father.

Then my uncle and later my guru, Swami Paramananda, came back to India after fifteen years of absence. He was Swami Vivekananda's youngest disciple, and had been sent to America. I was five when I first saw him in 1911. So we were really meeting for the first time. My father asked Swami Paramananda to take me out of India, saying, "We've already ruined her life; let her go." When my father heard me crying, he said, "Mother (that's what he called me), don't cry. You are doing penance for your parents' sin." He insisted that Swami Paramananda take me right then. But I was torn; where was my duty? I belonged to my husband's family. I waited for direction. Swami Paramananda saw me in this conflict, and said, "You'll have to decide." He wouldn't make the decision for me. I cried and prayed. I was just nineteen.

Swami Paramananda was coming to our home for lunch to get my answer, and my sister asked me if I knew what I was going to do. I didn't. He came in and had me sit with him on a bench prepared for him. "Well, Gayatri?" he asked in English. Only then did I know. "I will go with you." Ever since, I have been living at the ashram in America. I became the youngest in the community. Swami Paramananda established the first women's order. I was the ninth woman celibate of the order. The rest were Western women, Christians, who wore Christian habits. He was an innovator, a liberal, and put a Western woman disciple, Sister Devamata, who was older than himself, on the platform to teach Vedanta in 1910. When he passed away suddenly, at fifty-six, we had been assisting him for years, and he appointed me as his successor, even though there were no other such women leaders in the Ramakrishna Order.

I have lived such a long time; I'll be completing sixty years of work in this country in 1986. I have learned that you do not judge; you try to understand. I had fifteen months of training with my teacher; he shared his own experiences during the fourteen years I lived with him in community. He knew I'd be entrusted with his work. I will never sit and dictate or judge. We try to practice equality—equality, too, between monastics and householders. Our duties differ; one is not necessarily more spiritual than the other. Equality between men and women. Equality between East and West. Swami Paramananda lived here for thirty-four years. I feel, as he did, that I am as close to America as I am to India. I have no sense of East and West. I belong to the world.

THE RED ROAD

When I first read the handwritten notes of Grandfather Gerald Red Elk's words in this section, sitting comfortably in my livingroom chair, I experienced something I had not experienced before. I had the distinct impression—though well aware I was reading a transcript of a conversation that had happened twenty years before— that I was being addressed, twenty years later. More than that, that others were being addressed who were not in that retreat space either—future generations of Native Americans and still others I could not guess. Try as I might, I could not read the transcript without this impression.

When I began the actual editing, it was clear that the reader was going to have a tough time following these words, which from paragraph to paragraph could seem wholly unrelated. So I decided to break them up into discrete topics as I had done with the rest of the notes from 1984, but I did so with a heavy heart and an objection from my conscience. What else could I do? I resigned myself to it.

Later, over lunch with Tania Leontov, I told her of my impression of Red Elk's time-transcending, multivocal communication, and my guilt feelings over somehow disrupting it. To my eternal delight, she said, "That man was outside of time; he talked that way, and I have no doubt that this may have been happening." And then to my surprise, she added, "I think you should put it back together and let it stand as is with an explanatory note about your impressions."

Thus I have reconstructed Grandfather Red Elk's words from the original notes and have attempted to preserve them as accurately as was possible.

Among the Lakota Sioux, the "Red Road" is the straight path running north and south between Purity and the Source of All. In the words that follow, I believe Grandfather Gerald Red Elk and Father Thomas Keating describe the Red Road as they have walked it. I have kept their words together, just as they were spoken that first day of the conference, because they seem to be cut from the same cloth, as it were, reflecting the deep commitment and courage required to walk the spiritual path. Father Keating generously helped me to reconstruct his words from that day, and I can only pray that I have done equal justice to Grandfather Red Elk's words.

Grandfather Red Elk referred several times to an imminent "catastrophe" in those first two years of the conference, which he stressed might be avoided by our prayer and return to the Red Road. He suggested that the gathering of these people at Snowmass was one step in avoiding that fate. One hopes that such a fate was avoided in the intervening years, but perhaps we should see it only as a "parole," given the many terrible conflicts in our world; may we all follow the Red Road as Grandfather Red Elk advised. (N. M-Y.)

Grandfather Gerald Red Elk: If we don't share our sacred experiences, others won't know what we are really about . . . we are supposed to share and teach!

Long ago, my people were told what the white race would be like, what they would do, and it all happened as they predicted. So we had to adapt to a dual way of life, living the way of the white man, while also trying to retain our freedom, and keeping our own ways. During World War II, when I was a young man, I served this country in the war . . . because, if God permits war, one must take a stand either on the side of positivism or negativism. My friends and I all made a vow before we went to war. . . . If we came back alive, we would live the way our people were taught, we would live by our traditions. So we prayed this prayer with our hands on a tree of life, which was God Itself; we asked for wisdom, health, and life. . . . When you put your hand on a tree like that, you know God has put me here on this planet, in this form; I can't be anything else; I can learn other ways, but I am supposed to be who I am. So we promised we would live by our traditions if we returned.

But when we came back we did not do as we promised . . . we turned to alcohol, thinking that would help us, but it only destroyed us. When I finally got sick from all the anger, the hatred, and the alcohol, it was an answer to my wife's prayers. As I came close to death, I prayed again, "If You give me a second chance, I will love my fellow man, and truly live by the old ways." After that, the Star People, the Mystery, the Moving Stones came to me. They are spirits who come to help us to live and to understand. One came to my house then; he was half red and half blue. I had him for five years before I showed him to another person.

We always pray to the Creator first, then to the four directions, Mother Earth, and the Universe. But we ask permission for other deities to help us. We do this with red cloth and incense together. So, this stone began to glow and said to me, "I came because you are living the ancient ways; I came to help." You must always remember, there is a Supreme God, but these are His workers. I realized then that I had to live the life of what the teachings are: to be humble, generous, to have charity, and to always try not to lie—this is the Way of the Pipe.

You must acknowledge the Thunderbird People—the People seated in the West who come in April and leave in October. A holy man said to me that I am supposed to be a medicine man. This was important . . . : we have to steer the young in the right direction. They must know who they really are before they can help their fellow man. And you have got to want to do it; not just for experience's sake. Only then are you given the wisdom and knowledge, only then can you understand the mysteries. Sometimes the mysteries are simple.

There is always a reason why we do things, and we have to humble ourselves and accept everything *as it is*; that is how we learn. You must respect others' way of belief and praying, but remember that you are *you*. If you live the teachings, you'll be helped. Whatever we do or say, we create our own problems when we offend others. You live in harmony if you see all things in harmony—Jesus is "Father God," and His father is "Grandfather God"—God talks to every one of His people through prophets. Learn to be positive about this.

My people went back to the Sun Dance. We have to share our knowledge with everyone now. They dance, they meditate, they participate, and God has movement. The drum is the heartbeat of Mother Earth. God wants the people to unite and to accept one another. We all climb the mountain, but we take different paths.

We give our children special names in our language. We do things the way we were taught because it creates a discipline, even in the smallest etiquette of life. We call each other by our relationship, not by name. Otherwise, it is an insult. We are reviving respect now. But we must live the life ourselves, or it won't be revived. Every two hundred years comes the young rebel. The hippie movement was the two-hundredth–year rebellion. The hippies went on the positive side, so our civilization wasn't destroyed. Now we are coming back to life. The eagles started coming when we went back to the old ways. . . . His sign to us.

A powwow is a gathering of tribes every seven years—a council lodge to express feelings, to redo laws, and to look at our ways. And this is necessary. When you live *the life*, you elevate yourself. You believe God really exists. You acknowledge Him every day. Then He will show you things. He shows you through your interactions with other people. It is truly mystical! God sends moisture when He approves a religious gathering. When we are in unison here together, we feel good and can accomplish something. Twelve, the number in this group, is a sacred number.

When my people meditate, we go out in the hills. There are sacred spots there. *This* place is sacred. Offer incense, red cloth, and tobacco, and the writings will come out when you go to the sacred rocks. We ask the rock, "Whatever You show us, give us understanding of what it means, and what we are to do." The symbols that come out on the rock are the same as those that can be found in Hindu temples.

There is a big catastrophe coming and we must be taught to be strong in our beliefs. We must learn to live off the land. We must unite and help one another to survive. We must pray hard that all Humanity will survive. These things make us realize that He exists and make us do the right thing. He must know that we are trying in earnest. Then He shows us signs through people and things. If you really want to understand, you will be given the wisdom. It is for you.

The Hopis have in their history that the Tibetans came and taught them three thousand years ago. It was prophesied that when they come back, the end of this civilization is in sight. In the past, a great civilization was about to be destroyed. They called in the Star People to come and save them. Was it the Tibetans? Our teachings are so similar. The same as Buddhists and Jewish people. We've studied them carefully, and they are the same. We believe in reincarnation also. More and more Star People are appearing among our people. When I talked with Chögyam Trungpa Rinpoche, we saw a lightning bolt with five different colors; . . . the Buddha was made by lightning, it is thought.

Father Thomas Keating: We are also told in our tradition that we must *pray* to avoid these catastrophes. It is part of the mystery of the spiritual journey.

When I was eighteen, I decided to become a monk. So I looked for a difficult order and found the Trappists. My parents were very upset and angry. But I found myself romantically in love with God and had to do it. This was just as World War II was beginning for America, but I was being told, "This war does not involve you." So I was deferred and entered a strict form of monastic life. It was a difficult and austere life, but my will was determined to pursue the contemplative life at any cost . . . and I nearly lost my physical life. I was ordained a priest, and later I served as abbot. The abbot is at the center of tensions in a community, which often reflects the tensions of the larger society. Whatever he does, he can't win.

After the war, I traveled to Italy, and had what I can only describe as a mystical experience in a World War II cemetery there. As I looked at all the crosses and stars of David, I realized beyond any doubt that many of those who had lost their lives were somehow present with me there. I entered the monastery to pray for them, and somehow they appreciated what I had done, and the life I was leading. I seemed to have affected their destiny by following mine. Entering into God's plan is infinitely vaster than anything we can imagine. These men seemed like friends and brothers, alive to me. They seemed to say, "Now we'll help you in the 'war' you are engaged in."

My vision and concept of God, the Church, and my vocation were shattered step by step over the years. The meaning of the universe is sacrifice. The essence of the spiritual journey is to let go of everything, including one's life and life work. Even Christ had to let go of his intimate relationship with the Father. On the cross, he cries out, "Why do I have to be alienated from You!" The sense of separation from God goes with sin and influences everything we think or do. The willingness to be transformed means letting go of the false self. The latter is the hardest thing we have to do in this life. The death of the false self is the goal. Total self-surrender is resurrection. Even our spiritual path has to be left behind. In "The Story of the Jumping Mouse," the mouse becomes an eagle only when it no longer has eyes to see the path. God's plan is so long-range for each of us, yet perfect. How mysterious are its turns! The only certainty is that there isn't any.

THE COURAGE OF THE PATH

In this section, Pema Chödrön shows how dialogue is inherent in the basic curiosity of the Buddhist path and the Shambhala training of Chögyam Trungpa Rinpoche, where nothing is avoided or excluded, where one simply works with reality as it is. (N. M-Y.)

Ane Pema Chödrön: In his autobiography, *Born in Tibet*, Chögyam Trungpa Rinpoche describes his choice to jump into Western culture, and to know its true mind. Raised to be abbot from childhood, he was attempting to transplant the essence of the Tibetan

Buddhist teachings in the West. For him, the main characteristic of that was to work wholeheartedly with the existing situation, to get to know things so fully that one might perceive the "gateless" quality of things. The point is to work with the immediacy of one's situation, including the environment.

For us, the path includes curiosity and inquisitiveness. We are always gravitating toward challenge, and doing this with courage, learning in the process how not to be threatened by other points of view. We overcome the notion that things have to be a certain way. You just work with a situation as it is . . . one hundred percent flexible, open and available.

Often you feel you are in way over your head, but how else are you going to grow? So in this path, you develop respect for thinking big. This is the way of enlightenment. There is no better place and no better moment than now.

In Trungpa Rinpoche's Shambhala Training, the focus is on the reality of life as it is, basic goodness and the power of human potential. There is an emphasis on society, that the individual's journey is not just a personal attainment, but serves to influence world karma in a positive way, trying to uplift all of human society. We must cultivate openness, bravery, warriorship. Materialism and the tendency to be too comfortable is the enemy; seeking comfort and avoiding pain.

LIFE AND SPIRITUAL LIFE

In this section we have an excerpt of dialogue on the value of spiritual traditions and spiritual exemplars in general. (N. M-Y.)

Ane Pema Chödrön: We need mindfulness of even the smallest details of our lives. Be mindful of where you put things, of how they are cared for; care for your shoes is as important as attaining enlightenment.

Why is there need for the monastery? It is a part of a whole society. It has enormous power to inspire people to make a wholehearted commitment to what they're doing; it reminds us of the power of commitment, and serves as a model of commitment. And it preserves certain traditions that require continuity.

Swami Buddhananda: Yes, it is a training ground for showing others how to spiritualize everything that they do. In that way, there are fewer dichotomies in their lives between the spiritual and the material.

Rabbi Rami Shapiro: There is a Hasidic anecdote that says, "I didn't go to the rebbe to learn new Torah, I went to see how he tied his shoelaces." We need to have a spiritual life modeled for us, to learn how to tie our shoelaces with reverence. The dichotomy between spiritual and material is in our heads.

Imam Bilal Hyde: In Sufism, there is an emphasis on being able to be in retreat even within the noise of a pressing crowd, as one is at the Ka'aba. On the outside, you would simply appear to be with people, but on the inside you are attached to no one but the Beloved.

SURRENDER, THE EGO, AND VULNERABILITY

This section is probably the most representative of the general flow the dialogue and its energy, how it changes course naturally and follows the inspiration of the moment. (N. M-Y.)

Srimata Gayatri Devi: You must be totally surrendered. You are not supposed to know all the answers, and you ask no questions. The goal is yours; you don't even make a claim to it. You have to let go of wanting to know. But there can be no faith without basic knowledge. The basic knowledge is that . . . *That is* and that *you* are related to *That*.

Grandfather Gerald Red Elk: The eternal cycle of life is that you start as a child, you grow into a teenager, you become an adult, and finally you are an old person. You keep on learning and gaining experiences. We ask "What, why, and where?" But we must accept what They give us, and fulfill our purpose. If we don't surrender, we'll always be in doubt. God's intelligence is endless, as is this universe. We will always keep going on—the baby faces east, the teenager faces south, the adult with children faces west, and the holy people with white hair who have gained all wisdom face north.

Srimata Gayatri Devi: According to Sri Ramakrishna, once you have "arrived," you can leave the Earth. But there are those who don't leave; they no longer live for themselves. They are kept in the body. That is the bodhisattva ideal—not seeking our own salvation or liberation. With *moksha* and *mukti*, "liberation," you have attained everything you want. But still, you are not free by your own choice. Surrender is letting go, even after achieving; . . . you only know that you are being used. Only rare souls can render that kind of service. Most are caught up in their own achievement and attainment: *Nitya mukta* is one who is already free but comes back to serve, the bodhisattva; *sadhansiddha* struggles to attain; *hatathsiddha* has sudden illumination; and *kripasiddha* has Grace; God just frees them. God's nature is like a child, whimsical and unpredictable.

Grandfather Gerald Red Elk: Accept and surrender; just live it.

Srimata Gayatri Devi: We have this utterance, "Brahman is the Absolute; the knower of Brahman becomes like unto Brahman." They are merged. You and That become one.

Imam Bilal Hyde: Moses saw the bush and started to tread the path. Then he saw the fire, and heard, "I am that I am." So he took a leap into the fire to become part of it—he and the path are all the fire of Love.

Father Thomas Hopko: Serge of Saint Seraphim said, "God is Love. Christ is the son of His Love. The Holy Spirit is the communication of Their Love."

Ane Pema Chödrön: When there is no self, what's left? One must let go of the attachment to no self. There are five primordial energies—earth, air, fire, water, and space—from which all comes. Our four seasons (plus space) correspond to these. As long as there are notions of self, these energies are experienced as obstacles. But when there is no self, wisdom shines through them. You don't throw anything out on the spiritual path. We value our qualities, even if they seem destructive. Aggression sees all things threatening its survival. Wisdom is just "seeing."

Rabbi Rami Shapiro: The "I," or the individual ego, in Hebrew is called *ani*. And in kabbalah, Jewish mysticism, God is called *ain*, "Nothing." Two different words using the same three letters; in kabbalah, having the same letters suggests a relationship, and just a slight shift in the letters can create a new reality. So it is said when we turn the *ani* into *ain*, we are able to see the universe through God's eyes.

Father Thomas Hopko: Yes, the egoic "false self" is not the same as the ego on the path. Suppose the "false self" has died?

Srimata Gayatri Devi: The basic ego is just the I-sense—*aham*. It can't be destroyed; it shouldn't be destroyed. You operate through it. But its negative associations must be transformed. There is an immature ego and a ripe ego. For this, a sense of values is critical. What is high? We must acknowledge that *atman* has first place; it controls the ego. It is God in us. Jnana says, "I am That," "Thou art That." Sri Ramakrishna says that that attitude is a little dangerous so long as we have so many drives, tendencies of a self that is not conquered or self-subjugated. Bhakta says, "I don't want to be sugar; I want to taste sugar." Taste Him; be in relationship. Your ego becomes a servant, a child, or a friend. There are different relationships that can be developed with the Divine—parent–child, friend–friend, master–servant, beloved–lover. This last is the highest and most difficult. All senses, desires and egotism must be conquered. Let God direct your ego. Neither belittle it nor glorify it. Give it its rightful place, and let it be the tool. Self is death. Truth is life. We must return to pure teaching.

Father Thomas Hopko: When the "false self" dies, there is no choice anymore. Do we have a choice? Or do we discover who we are and what is our way?

Father Thomas Keating: It is not effort or choice, but *consent*.

Imam Bilal Hyde: My sheikh has said, "The pen has written and the ink is dry." I know that the pen has written, but I act as if it hasn't; we act as if we had a choice. We should pray as if we were going to die the next minute, and work as if we had eternity.

Swami Buddhananda: Maya is a "seeming" reality.

Rabbi Rami Shapiro: In Judaism, we speak about *bittul ha-yesh*, "the annihilation of existence," or of everything that exists. The idea is to destroy "the known." The known isn't It. When you have destroyed the known, *It* is what is left. Absolute vulnerability is absolute strength.

Father Thomas Keating: That moment of absolute weakness is a marvelous gift, a journey into greater and greater interior freedom.

Imam Bilal Hyde: There is a joke that says, "A Muslim is either a person who can get all five prayers in daily . . . or one who feels guilty about not getting them in!"

Srimata Gayatri Devi: What is the greatest wonder? That people don't believe in death for themselves. We are sheaths. Letting go frees us from attachment, the clinging to life. "Lead us from the unreal to the Real." You don't become heartless when you transcend; grief is human. You love, you care, you miss. Even the great sage who knew the Truth cried at the death of his son. To suffer, and then to transcend suffering, that is it. You know the truth and accept it, but that doesn't mean your heart doesn't ache.

Father Thomas Keating: Christ wept about Lazarus. . . . He wept in Gethsemane.

Imam Bilal Hyde: The Sufis say, "Die before you die." Dying is a tearing of the veil to get nearer to the Light within. It is necessary in moving toward our goal. Rumi said, "The path of the seeker is a bloody path." Everything passes away in this world except for the face of God, gloriously shining. Our suffering is commensurate with our attachment. As soon as we let go, surrender to total surrender, it leads to peace. The heart of every believer is between the two fingers of God; when He contracts them, we cry, when He opens them, we laugh.

COMMITMENT AND ATTAINMENT

Srimata Gayatri Devi talks here of the radical responsibility one must take for one's own spiritual life. (N. M-Y.)

Srimata Gayatri Devi: There is always form, tradition and structure. But the most important factor is the individual, no matter what our lifestyle or tradition. We have a choice of how we apply what we believe in. Are we allowing the Truth to take us over? And do we accept all the challenges that come? We can accept them, or we can blame others and circumstances.

We have the concept of Cosmic *lila*, the "play" or sport of the Divine. You can't separate the relative from the Absolute if you are consciously relating to the Divine. The real problem is with ourselves, how far we want to go, and what we have as our highest aspiration. Are we are willing to do everything necessary? How much confidence in the Self would it take to attain the highest goal? Your orientation has to be very clear. It doesn't matter what others do. What we do is most important. You become committed. Some go very far, while others get stuck or stop in the middle. Thakur [Sri Ramakrishna] said, "Everyone can attain the Highest. The high goal is to become consciously divine, to be part and parcel of It."

We must learn to love each other because of the *atman*, the soul, which dwells within. It is our attraction to the One within which makes us love. What you are is much more important than words or garments. Ralph Waldo Emerson wrote, "What you are speaks so loudly, I cannot hear what you are saying." If you are on the spiritual journey, eventually you will arrive. Lord Buddha is called *tathagata* in Pali, "one who has arrived there." One who embraces the life of holiness has tremendous responsibility. As one moves on, one's task is self-discipline and restraint on every level. One's aspiration is to "get there." You can't force yourself. Lord Krishna in the Bhagavad Gita says that "among thousands of human beings, scarcely one comes after Him. And among thousands of faithful strivers, scarcely one knows me in truth." It is not an easy path. Of the thousands of followers in organizations, how many are really strivers? The majority is caught up in their personal lives, drives, and desires. We are not all in the same place. In the West, everyone is equal, on one level. On the developmental level, spiritually, we are not. You'll be there someday. Don't be disheartened. You go through many stages. Your experiences help you make your end.

As human beings, our goal is to use this human birth to attain union with the One, who dwells within inseparably. Religion is the way through that we will attain. When we return in a different body, we bring in with us impressions and imprints of our previous experiences, associations and contacts. We are souls. This particular incarnation is related to now. The future depends upon what we do here.

Rabbi Rami Shapiro: A Messiah candidate once appeared in Yemen. The bewildered Jewish populace wrote to Moses Maimonides asking what to do. He suggested that they ask the man to perform a miracle. They did, and he promised that if they all gathered at dawn the next morning, they could cut off his head, and he would put it back on again. They gathered and cut off his head and there it remained. The only comment that could be heard was from his mother: "You start, but you never finish anything!"

MANTRA

I have chosen to preserve this fragment because it is a good example of the value of peer-to-peer dialogue among spiritual directors, and the honing of that direction. (N. M-Y.)

Swami Buddhananda: A guru tests the *chela* a lot before mantra initiation, because it amplifies one's nature, both the light and the dark. So the guru makes certain that one has the commitment and strength to deal with what arises.

Srimata Gayatri Devi: The word "Jesus" is a mantra. The word or name that you have chosen must be natural to you. The word, being an expression of thought, is tremendously powerful. The mantra releases the unconscious. If there is no discipline, you are blown away by negatives. Some sacred words or sounds are invested with power by their very nature.

A SACRED LAND

This section treats the topic of cultural exclusivity, ecology, and the importance of dealing with the American landscape as a sacred landscape, mapped from time immemorial by the native peoples of the continent. (N. M-Y.)

Swami Buddhananda: Only in the uniting of spiritual power can healing take place. Before the sacred hoop of the Native Americans was tragically broken, Crazy Horse had a vision of its breaking, and when he told this vision to his mother, she suggested, "Maybe our hoop is too small." When the hoop is rejoined, it will include all of the people. Then we will know that we are living in a sacred land. We don't need to look for another. We've abused this land because we haven't understood its sacredness. In America, the Native Americans know all the sacred places of this land and why they are sacred. The Native

Americans held this land pristinely. All belonged to God. Nothing more was taken from the land than was needed.

Srimata Gayatri Devi: How will people in America learn that this country is sacred land? Pilgrimages? Will they do it if their leaders do it?

Grandfather Gerald Red Elk: When God wants it, a group of people will go. This whole planet is sacred, but this is His tortoise continent. This land was His very choice land. He populated it with everything, and with people from different lands. Seven clans. His number is seven.

You *make* a place hallowed. You go into it barefooted. God is Mother Earth. Everything that moves and grows has a soul . . . rocks, mountains and trees . . . they all talk. The land is all ours. We are all His children and He wants us to live as such. The people who came to this continent are special people. He allowed them to come. It is a land of plenty. There is plenty here for everybody, enough for balance, and it is all sacred.

BLESSING

The conference ended with this blessing from Srimata Gayatri Devi. (N. M-Y.)

Srimata Gayatri Devi: Send peace in all directions. *Shanti.* May all beings be happy. May all beings be free from affliction. May all beings see glorious days. May no one suffer or be sad. You must be concerned with all humanity and the whole Earth; become globally concerned. You must be identified with each soul. Pray immediately for anyone you see afflicted. The atmosphere, the commitment, and the individual spiritual life here at Snowmass are powerful; you don't realize the influence of this place. It generates a tremendous force in the world. Let's embrace everybody, everywhere. This place should radiate this peace, goodwill and love. Our peace is more important than our words. Let's come together with one another. The more we share, the better it is for all of us. One people, one humanity.

CHAPTER SIX

SPIRITUAL PRACTICES: EXCERPTS FROM SNOWMASS II

ANANDA ASHRAM, 1985

Based on the notes of Srimata Sudha Puri, taken at Ananda Ashram, La Crescenta, California, on Tuesday, May 7, 1985

WHICH SPIRITUAL PRACTICE HAS BEEN MOST HELPFUL TO YOU?

Srimata Gayatri Devi: Our life is action balanced by contemplation. In my early days in the ashram, I had much less time to give to contemplation, and I felt nervous that I couldn't do justice to my spiritual practice. So I told my teacher, Swami Paramananda, that I couldn't meditate or lose myself during the periods of meditation because I had to be so active. And he said, "Don't worry, as long as you have faith and devotion, all is well."

This is what I understood by faith: I know that Reality IS. Whether I can communicate with It or feel Its presence or not doesn't change that fact. Prayer to me is an attitude of intimacy, so I could say, "Lord, I don't have time right now to sit and think of You, but I know that You will understand; *I know that You ARE*, whether or not I see You or experience You in my spiritual practices." This led me to have a habitual awareness of the Divine: He is and you are; He is first and you are second; everything is directed to Him. When I eat, I am offering the food to the Divine Mother. When I greet the sun each morning, I am grateful to her. My devotion I expressed through action within the community. I have always tried to follow the Bhagavad Gita's injunction: "Whatever you do, whatever you eat, whatever you offer as oblation, whatever you give and whatever austerities you perform, O son of Kunti, do that as an offering to Me" (9:27). Everything is directed toward the Divine; . . . surrender is my path, an acceptance of life as it is, accompanied by a constant repetition of the mantra under the breath.

But also, because my attitude toward the Divine is one of a child to a Mother. . . . I have made many demands of God for help: "Please do it! Nothing is impossible to you! Please, what is it to you? You are omnipotent!" This is our right, and is a valuable practice.

Father Thomas Keating: The practice of stillness . . . of body, mind and heart . . . is an entrance into interior silence that opens one up to the Divine Presence as It manifests Itself. This silence and stillness permeates the mind, the brain, the wholeness of one's being, and transforms it. I find that this practice brings about an inner tranquility, harmony and watchfulness and leads to a more intense awareness of both the interior and exterior life; it results in a surrender to the Providential Process of Life and enables one to flow in peaceful quietude with whatever one encounters. Each day, I find more and more delight and spiritual renewal in this practice.

I have also found a great solace in *Lectio Divina*, contemplative reading of the Gospels. For exoteric practices such as this can often lead to the awakening of the esoteric, allowing one to reinterpret tradition in light of emerging consciousness.

Rabbi Rami Shapiro: I worship through the four dimensions of my being: doing, feeling, thinking and being. Doing is the physical: attention to diet, walking, watching my breath while out hiking; I have always been profoundly affected by contact with the natural world. Feeling is watching myself in interaction, observing the emotions that arise. Thinking is used in the study of Torah and the spiritual literature of the world. Being is worship in stillness.

Tania Leontov: *Tonglen* is a meditative practice of exchange, exchanging oneself for another. Through visualization and feelings, changing places, taking the pain of another and sending clarity and light to that person. It can be done for someone that you know, a stranger, or even for a whole situation. You sit in meditation posture, visualizing the person or situation with which you wish to relate; flash on the negative aspect of the situation and its environmental feel, the abstract quality of the negative situation. Then, you connect and feel yourself in touch with light and clarity and begin to alternate between the negativity and the clarity, taking in the issue or the pain and sending out clarity, sanity and healing. This practice works on your capacity for compassion, and begins to develop *prajna*, precise understanding.

Roger La Borde: The most helpful practice for me is simply recognizing that there is no place but *here*. There is no path; I simply have to pay attention to right now, to what I am dealing with *here*. There is no place to go, nowhere to run to, no savior, and no heaven; I just have to deal with who I Am.

Ane Pema Chödrön: For me it is the sitting practice of meditation emphasizing the basic *nowness* . . . this moment being all there is. This awareness ripens three aspects of the mind: 1) precision, the ability to pay attention; 2) gentleness, the heart quality, the soft touch; and 3) openness and willingness to never have your questions answered—inquisitiveness unrequited—*letting go*.

Imam Bilal Hyde: In my tradition, we have *zikr*, "remembrance," remembrance of *Allah hu akbar*, "God who is greater!" Remembrance, in its most universal sense, is praise and thanksgiving, resonating in every atom of the universe. For me, the foundation of remembrance is the practice of the five daily prayers, *salat*, which remind the Sufi to look at the Beloved's face. Remembrance in the path of perfection is to "worship God as if you see Him; for, even if you don't see Him, surely He sees you." Surrender is to remember that *that Essence is first . . . I am second*. I surrender to the object of remembrance. I walk in complete trust of the Divine plan. It is not a mechanical remembrance, but complete trust and surrender to the Beloved. This is the natural disposition of the universe . . . sincere remembrance.

Father George Timko: I practice "the crucifixion of heart," or living with impossible situations for God's sake. Total surrender into the Providence of God. Trying to be grateful in all circumstances.

Prayer in Orthodoxy is communion, not communicating. Contemplation is watching and attentiveness, being watchful of one's inner reality.

Grandfather Gerald Red Elk: When I was young, I didn't realize that I was on the Black Road of rebellion. I wanted the Star People to help me to understand, to help me find the Red Road. And They came and touched me. I wanted to love my fellow man, because I had hate in my heart. I asked Them to take my jealousy and prejudice away. I wished to love others no matter who or what they were; to be the person I really was supposed to be, and to live it.

I pray all the time; I ask forgiveness for all the evil thoughts that come into my mind; I ask that they be taken away. Day and night I pray. I pray within myself all the time, and it works, it works for me. I overcome by praying silently. I vowed to live and to love, and to help my fellow man regardless of who they are. I do it . . . not just say it. I am trying all the time to have action and not just words. I accept things as they come. I am glad. I give thanks. *They* acknowledge things that you do that are positive; pray and it shall be given to you. Prayer is most important. Then we put it into action. I surrendered myself, I prayed, it all turns out. I can never forget that They exist. If I did, I'd be committing blasphemy.

Pray in a room all by yourself when you first wake up. Pray with the Morning Star, heralding day that is going to come. Be thankful for seeing another day, and ask for guidance. In the evening, give thanks for that day, and be thankful that They will watch over you in the darkness. Go into the hills and find your education. Watch the actions of birds and other animals—ants are great teachers to us. You have to sing your songs four times to Grandfather God and three to Father God.

Swami Buddhananda: Prayer and meditation are central for me. They brought me to surrender . . . to letting go. My greatest spiritual discipline began with noninstigation of action, accepting whatever work is given me to do, and doing it with total attention. Everything in my life dictates the next assignment; I listen to what's presenting itself at any given moment. I do each task to the limit of my capacity, and trust implicitly that the Lord will add whatever is necessary to complete it.

CHAPTER SEVEN

SPIRITUAL AUTHORITY AND ETHICS: NOTES FROM SNOWMASS III

KARMÊ CHÖLING, 1986

Srimata Sudha Puri, Order of Ramakrishna Brahmavadin

SPIRITUAL AUTHORITY

At the third Snowmass Conference, held at the Karmê Chöling Meditation Center in Vermont, we discussed two subjects of concern to religious groups and spiritual seekers from all traditions. The first was "Spiritual Authority: What is it? Who has it?" Some of our comments on this question are given below:

- Ultimate Reality is the supreme "authority."
- We give authority to Holy Scriptures based upon the direct experience of their depth, and as an expression of our confidence in their ability to help others to reach the greater authority . . . Self-Knowledge.
- Spiritual authority is a potential within each of us. The individual soul is none other than the Divine. The experience of this comes through no teacher or institution; it comes from within. Genuine presence emerges when nothing is in the way.
- Spiritual authority is only possible if you have deeply experienced what you have learned. We often give authority to other people through titles, degrees and positions, and while individual teachers may have knowledge, ability and power to influence others, the origin of spiritual authority is based in an experience of Ultimate Reality.

- The level of one's spiritual authority depends on the degree of manifestation of pure spirit, and authority has a particular aspect at each level.
- It is good to respect authority and to accept guidance from one in whom one has confidence, but it is not good to give one's power away. Followers consent to recognize authority, but should be discerning in how they do this.
- The root meaning of authority is "service." As an authority, a teacher is an instrument. Ramakrishna's example of fencing a young tree to protect it until it grows strong enough to stand entirely without support is a good illustration of this service.
- Summary: when authority is used in selfless service, the results are enlightening. When authority it used for power and control, it unquestionably corrupts.

THE SOURCE OF GOODNESS IN SPIRITUALITY AND ETHICS

Our second subject and the theme of our public session was "The Source of Goodness in Spirituality and Ethics." After our initial private discussion, we realized the need to carefully define "ethics," and direct our attention to specific spiritual development in relation to this rather broad concept. Below are some of our comments on this question:

- Ethics are systems of social behavior designed to address the potential chaos and randomness of individual behavior in group or communal relationships.
- Many ethical patterns develop directly from environmental as well as social conditions. These variables may change quite drastically with time, place and human condition.
- When an individual, a group or even a nation becomes dysfunctional at certain levels, it is generally due to a breakdown in moral and ethical systems. These, in turn, require reevaluation and corrective measures, a reformation to prevent chaos and complete downfall, such as has been witnessed throughout history.

- In the context of goodness and spirituality, social ethics should create a condition which nurtures the greatest amount of good for the most people in any given time, place or circumstance.
- Individual spiritual ethics and moral injunctions are generally accepted as fundamental in the "path" or "way" that an aspirant may follow to expanded consciousness and enlightenment. It is important to note, however, that many people have a highly developed sense of ethics and morality without identification with any spiritual or religious system.
- Spiritual ethics (ethics connected with Divine revelation or inspiration) are generally more refined and supersede common social ethics. These codes require a greater degree of awareness, discipline and social sensitivity from the person or persons who adhere to them.
- Corporate common sense can help one discern "the wheat from the chaff" in one's private revelations. That is to say, a spiritual aspirant may use a peer group to test their private revelations, to see if they reflect the group's common purpose and intent.
- The Snowmass Conference participants consider life on Earth to be a spiritual journey whether taken with awareness or not.
- The Snowmass Conference participants agreed to bypass specific contemporary issues such as abortion, arms manufacturing and the like in order to avoid unnecessary heated encounters with our conference audience. As a group in the public, we try not to give the appearance of a committee of experts who have come together to solve the world's problems. We certainly acknowledge the conditions of our time, but feel the solution lies more in the realm of personal transformation. Each "healthy" individual then accepts the responsibility of helping others out of confusion. The healthy and holy ones are most deeply in touch with the wellspring, or source, of goodness that flows from the very center of their beings.
- In commenting on the morality of our time, which seems extremely lax relative to other periods in history, we felt that the dark side of human nature can best be examined with a view to transforming that potential energy, rather than suppressing it. By coming to terms with our humanness, and accepting ourselves

with a degree of kindness, we might work in a positive way to re-
create our lives. If darkness is to be viewed as a super-imposition
over our basic goodness, then it is our responsibility to make an
effort to remove it.

- We concede that persons attracted by the desire for personal
  transformation or spiritual liberation have in some way received
  a special "grace." Although the word "grace" implies Divine
  intervention from a source outside ourselves, we use it in the
  broader sense that includes a condition granted by the higher
  nature of one's own mind.

- Concerning the "Source of Goodness," we were inclined to refer
  back to our term "Ultimate Reality," which we perceive as the
  ground essence of all being, and that which is beyond. As our
  lives are penetrated, sustained, and are given meaning by this
  Reality, it must be the very source of goodness.

- The recorded lives of the great Masters and Saints indicate that
  it is possible to return to the state of perfection from which we
  were created. Through disciplines, intense desire for transcendence and faith in our higher natures, we may experience what
  they have known. What is possible for one is inherent in all.

- Ultimately, each individual is responsible for self-transformation,
  and is held to account for their choices in all matters concerning
  morals and ethics. All of our diverse religious systems agree that
  action reaps its own reward according to kind.

CHAPTER EIGHT

THE POINTS OF UNIQUENESS: NOTES FROM SNOWMASS XVIII

ST. BENEDICT'S MONASTERY, 2004

These "points" were collected by Rev. Donald Postema from responses given by the Snowmass Conference members on March 26, 2004, in answer to the questions: "What makes the Snowmass Conference work? And what makes it unique?"

- We speak to each other; we are not presenting to the public, and that allows for honest interchange, questioning, feedback and safe challenge. Members are speaking *from* a tradition and not *for* a tradition. While emerging from our respective traditions, we really represent our own experience and opinion rather than the tradition in many cases. One is encouraged to represent one's own tradition authentically, but no less one's own personal experience.
- Environment is important: the environment should be spacious and warmly hospitable; we were hosted at our respective centers when possible. We found that a nonsacred environment was detrimental to the meetings. The accommodations were comfortable and the food very good; physical comforts added to the sense of well being and camaraderie.
- The original group had an exceptionally high number of advanced spiritual people whose humility and clarity modeled this for the rest of us. Their brilliance and compassion were beyond the dogma of the religions they represented, which helped tame the minds of the others. It has continued to be a spiritually experienced group, in whom daily life and spiritual practice have begun to integrate.

- We all started with a degree of open-mindedness; there were no hidebound traditionalists. Everyone is somewhat conversant with other paths, and so we are able to converse and ask significant questions. It is a pleasure to have people learned enough to go into depth, and that leads to a cumulative depth of the group. It is good for us, as leaders, to get together in a peer group where we aren't teaching, but sharing as peers.

- The model is not one of giving a presentation; we drop roles and have a rich and honest sharing on multiple levels. Members are "practitioners" in the group, not hierarchs or theologians, and they are asked to share from that standpoint.

- We discovered the need to get acquainted at the level of friendship before sharing the deeper meaning of the terms and concepts of our respective traditions.

- The relative stability of the group from year to year allowed for this friendship and intimacy, the ability to share from a personal standpoint, the willingness to take a risk with each other, and humor at one's own expense, a space even to be irreverent, where no subject is taboo. We feel safe, so we can question things. We aren't invincible, so we can serve as resources for each other. It has also allowed us to witness the growth and development of members over the years, which has been inspiring.

- In sharing and listening, one's own experience and spiritual practice become deepened. Entering into the experience of what helped other members of the group most in their spiritual journey was fruitful in our own lives.

- A sense of love has arisen among the members: mutual appreciation and love. That bond lasts over time, though we meet only once a year. Thus we have been deeply affected by the death of former members.

- We started out trying to see if there was anything we agreed upon as elements of our respective traditions. To our surprise there were a number of points on which we reached agreement. More than expected. We took our time and didn't "railroad" each other to agreement. It took four or five years. We then investigated points on which we disagreed, which was fruitful as well.

- We learned the importance of language, especially through the difficulty of communication between impersonal, nontheistic traditions and deeply personal, theistic traditions. We didn't gloss over the differences. There was a general willingness among the members to translate from one tradition to another.
- We sometimes find we are closer to representatives of other traditions than to some members of our own tradition.
- Meditating or sitting in quiet together for extended periods was very beneficial in uniting us at a deeper level.
- There is a "tasting" of each other's contemplative traditions, of each other's experience.
- We have been enriched by participating in the rituals of the various traditions.
- There is a space and willingness to listen in our dialogue. We have developed unspoken rules of engagement over the years. Inspired by interest, we have learned to allow others space to speak; but we haven't lapsed into mere polite acquiescence. We almost never heard an expression of contempt—challenge and humor, yes, but not contempt.
- A communal, tranquil and joyful state emerges from the meetings, not quantifiable or physical. A new, shared meditative consciousness emerged from the conjoining of many diverse traditions, greater and more profound than the sum of its parts. Our meetings give us a sense of hope to engage in the modern world of plurality, give a sense of positive possibility for the world.
- We find new and surprising things to share in each meeting, and there is a willingness to continue dialogue between sessions.
- We learn to associate the faces of real people with traditions; the traditions are no longer textbook abstractions.
- We invited a nonaligned member, an independent seeker not on a traditional path, into the group. This helped to keep us honest and challenged.
- We learned to speak of experience of the Ultimate Reality, rather than speaking about ideas. Ideas are used to express experience, and we are challenged at the level of experience by others.

- It has been exhilarating to hear hard questions about one's core beliefs; we have been stimulated to articulate our core beliefs so that they are understood by someone from a completely different tradition.
- One's tradition, beliefs and experiences are challenged not only by direct questions, but often by simply hearing a very different point of view or tradition explained by another member. We learned that we could be totally committed to our own traditions, and open at the same time to teaching from other traditions. We have assumptions shattered as we go deeper and deeper into sharing.
- Members understand their own core beliefs better and are often strengthened in their faith by dialogue. This is contrary to what people often think happens: that in interfaith dialogue, one either loses one's moorings or becomes wishy-washy in one's faith.
- There is a sense of commitment to a path of transformation, and once that happens, one plugs into a higher consciousness, a super-mind or common mind, not exactly God, but a higher unity of minds, like wholes within wholes within wholes. When someone says something, it comes more from the level of common mind, and that common mind or super-mind illumines the whole group without effort. The bond becomes indestructible, and we are able to access higher truths, coming from a higher intelligence that inspires the whole group at once.
- What we have accomplished has been carried back into our everyday lives, and directly affects our lives and communities.

AFTERWORD

FATHER THOMAS KEATING, OCSO

Many paths seek the Source. We call this the Absolute, Deus, God, Brahman, the Great Spirit, Ain Sof, Allah, Alaya and many other names, depending on our frame of reference. The term Ultimate Reality might best designate what all these words try to signify. All who seek to participate in Ultimate Reality are united in the same fundamental search. They relate to all of genuine value in every spiritual path. They resonate to human values wherever they can be found, whether in religions, science, art, friendship or service to others. True unity is thus expressed in pluralism: unity in the experience of the ultimate values of human life; pluralism in our response to these values in the concrete circumstances of life.

Those who seek Ultimate Reality perceive themselves as citizens of the Earth. Their first loyalty is to the entire human family. They transcend the particularities of race, nationality and religion without reacting against them or trying to destroy them. They recognize the profound human values that the world religions enshrine. They work to preserve and enhance these values, but not at the cost of dividing the fundamental unity of the human family. They belong to an emerging global community.

All seekers, especially adherents of the world religions, have an obligation to contribute to the cause of peace. In the past, and even now, ideological and religious differences sometimes have led and continue to lead to violence, injustice and persecution. Each tradition has developed teachings and practices designed to foster the full development of the human person. Common elements need to be identified, affirmed and made more available to the world community as powerful means of promoting understanding, compassion and harmony. Spiritual communion is the catalyst that facilitates cooperation on every level of global interaction.

The most precious value that we have in common is the accumulated experience of the spiritual journey. Over the centuries, seekers have discovered and lived its conditions, temptations, development and final integration. The wealth of personal experience of the transcendent is the historical grounding of the contemporary search. Spiritual seeking is not just a passing fad. As teachers of the various spiritual disciplines pool their common experiences, resources and insights, the benefit to contemporary seekers and to the world will be immense.

THE SNOWMASS CONFERENCES AND PARTICIPANTS

COMPILED BY DR. IBRAHIM GAMARD

SNOWMASS I

St. Benedict's Monastery, Snowmass, Colorado (October 21–24, 1984)

- Swami Buddhananda (Hindu, Vedanta, Ramakrishna Order)
- Ane Pema Chödrön (Buddhist, Tibetan Vajrayana, Karma Kagyü)
- Srimata Gayatri Devi (Hindu, Vedanta, Order of Ramakrishna Brahmavadin)
- Bernard Tetsugen Glassman Sensei (Buddhist, Zen, Soto School)
- Father Thomas Hopko (Christian, Russian Orthodox)
- Imam Bilal Hyde (Muslim, Sunni, Naqshbandi Sufi Order)
- Father Thomas Keating (Christian, Roman Catholic, Order of Cistercians of the Strict Observance)
- Tania Schwartz (Leontov) (Buddhist, Tibetan Vajrayana)
- Grandfather Gerald Red Elk (Native American, Yanktonai Lakota Sioux)
- Rabbi Rami Shapiro (Jewish, Reconstructionist)
- Dr. Douglas V. Steere (Christian, Quaker Society of Friends)
- Bhikshuni Yuen Yi (Buddhist, Chinese)

Observers
- Roger La Borde (Attendant to Grandfather Gerald Red Elk)
- Sister Sudha (Attendant to Srimata Gayatri Devi)
- Father Theophane Boyd (Christian, Roman Catholic, Order of Cistercians of the Strict Observance)
- Darrol Bryant

SNOWMASS II
Ananda Ashram, La Crescenta, California (May 5–9, 1985)

- Swami Buddhananda (Hindu, Vedanta, Ramakrishna Order)
- Ane Pema Chödrön (Buddhist, Tibetan Vajrayana, Karma Kagyü)
- Srimata Gayatri Devi (Hindu, Vedanta, Order of Ramakrishna Brahmavadin)
- Imam Bilal Hyde (Muslim, Sunni, Naqshbandi Sufi Order)
- Father Thomas Keating (Christian, Roman Catholic, Order of Cistercians of the Strict Observance)
- Roger La Borde (nonaligned)
- Tania Leontov (Buddhist, Tibetan Vajrayana)
- Rabbi Elisha Nattiv (Jewish)
- Grandfather Gerald Red Elk (Native American, Yanktonai Lakota Sioux)
- Rabbi Rami Shapiro (Jewish, Reconstructionist)
- Sister Sudha (Hindu, Vedanta, Order of Ramakrishna Brahmavadin)
- Sheikha Farah Takeshian (Muslim, Sufi)*
- Father George Timko (Christian, Eastern Orthodox)

* Imam Bilal Hyde invited Farah, a Muslim friend of his, because he thought she had much to contribute, and called her "Sheikha" to give her acceptance at the conference.

SNOWMASS III
*Karmê Chöling Buddhist Meditation Center, Barnet, Vermont
(May 5–9, 1986)*

- Swami Buddhananda (Hindu, Vedanta, Ramakrishna Order)
- Ane Pema Chödrön (Buddhist, Tibetan Vajrayana, Karma Kagyü)
- Srimata Gayatri Devi (Hindu, Vedanta, Order of Ramakrishna Brahmavadin)
- Father Thomas Keating (Christian, Roman Catholic, Order of Cistercians of the Strict Observance)

- Roger La Borde (nonaligned)
- Tania Leontov (Buddhist, Tibetan Vajrayana)
- Sister Sudha (Hindu, Vedanta, Order of Ramakrishna Brahmavadin)
- Father George Timko (Christian, Eastern Orthodox)

SNOWMASS IV
Sedona, Arizona (April 21–25, 1987)

- James Barnett (formerly Swami Buddhananda, non-aligned)
- Ane Pema Chödrön (Buddhist, Tibetan Vajrayana, Karma Kagyü)
- Srimata Gayatri Devi (Hindu, Vedanta, Order of Ramakrishna Brahmavadin)
- Reverend Robert B. Dunbar (Christian, Episcopalian)
- Father Thomas Keating (Christian, Roman Catholic, Order of Cistercians of the Strict Observance)
- Roger La Borde (nonaligned)
- Nettie Lujan (Native American, Taos Pueblo)
- Tania Leontov (Buddhist, Tibetan Vajrayana)
- Sister Sudha (Hindu, Vedanta, Order of Ramakrishna Brahmavadin)
- Carolyn Tawangyama (Native American, Hopi)
- Father George Timko (Christian, Eastern Orthodox)

Observer
- Carl Shelton (SHARE)

SNOWMASS V
Mount Holyoke College, Mount Holyoke, Massachusetts
(April 19–23, 1988)

- James Barnett (formerly Swami Buddhananda, nonaligned)
- Srimata Gayatri Devi (Hindu, Vedanta, Order of Ramakrishna Brahmavadin)

- Rabbi Dovid Din (Jewish, Hasidic)
- Reverend Robert B. Dunbar (Christian, Episcopalian)
- Dr. Ibrahim Gamard (Muslim, Sunni, Mevlevi Sufi Order)
- Gesshin Prabhasa Dharma Roshi (Buddhist, Zen, Rinzai School)
- Father Thomas Keating (Christian, Roman Catholic, Order of Cistercians of the Strict Observance)
- Roger La Borde (nonaligned)
- Tania Leontov (Buddhist, Tibetan Vajrayana)
- Nettie Lujan (Native American, Taos Pueblo)
- Reverend Donald H. Postema (Christian, Calvinist, Christian Reformed Church of North America)
- Sister Sudha (Hindu, Vedanta, Order of Ramakrishna Brahmavadin)
- Father George Timko (Christian, Eastern Orthodox)
- Carolyn Tawangyama (Native American, Hopi)

Observers
- Adele Millette (Christian, Roman Catholic)
- Connie Daniel

SNOWMASS VI
St. Benedict's Monastery, Snowmass, Colorado (May 1–5, 1989)

- James Barnett (formerly Swami Buddhananda, nonaligned)
- Ane Pema Chödrön (Buddhist, Tibetan Vajrayana, Karma Kagyü)
- Srimata Gayatri Devi (Hindu, Vedanta, Order of Ramakrishna Brahmavadin)
- Reverend Robert B. Dunbar (Christian, Episcopalian)
- Dr. Ibrahim Gamard (Muslim, Sunni, Mevlevi Sufi Order)
- Gesshin Prabhasa Dharma Roshi (Buddhist, Zen, Rinzai School)
- Father Thomas Keating (Christian, Roman Catholic, Order of Cistercians of the Strict Observance)
- Noel R. Knockwood (Native American, Micmac)
- Roger La Borde (nonaligned)
- Tania Leontov (Buddhist, Tibetan Vajrayana)

- Reverend Donald H. Postema (Christian, Calvinist, Christian Reformed Church of North America)
- Sister Sudha (Hindu, Vedanta, Order of Ramakrishna Brahmavadin)
- Father George Timko (Christian, Eastern Orthodox)

Observer
- Father Theophane Boyd (Christian, Roman Catholic, Order of Cistercians of the Strict Observance)

SNOWMASS VII
Bellarmine House, Cohasset, Massachusetts (May 8–12, 1990)

- James Barnett (formerly Swami Buddhananda, nonaligned)
- Ane Pema Chödrön (Buddhist, Tibetan Vajrayana, Karma Kagyü)
- Srimata Gayatri Devi (Hindu, Vedanta, Order of Ramakrishna Brahmavadin)
- Reverend Robert B. Dunbar (Christian, Episcopalian)
- Dr. Ibrahim Gamard (Muslim, Sunni, Mevlevi Sufi Order)
- Gesshin Prabhasa Dharma Roshi (Buddhist, Zen, Rinzai School)
- Father Thomas Keating (Christian, Roman Catholic, Order of Cistercians of the Strict Observance)
- Roger La Borde (nonaligned)
- Tania Leontov (Buddhist, Tibetan Vajrayana)
- Reverend Donald H. Postema (Christian, Calvinist, Christian Reformed Church of North America)
- Rabbi Schlomo Schwartz (Jewish, Hasidic, HaBaD)
- Sister Sudha (Hindu, Vedanta, Order of Ramakrishna Brahmavadin)
- Father George Timko (Christian, Eastern Orthodox)

Dinner Guests
- Ayya Khema (Buddhist, Theravada)
- Father John Martin (Christian, Roman Catholic, Maryknoll Order)

SNOWMASS VIII
Nada Hermitage, Spiritual Life Institute, Crestone, Colorado
(August 20–23, 1991)

- James Barnett (formerly Swami Buddhananda, nonaligned)
- Ane Pema Chödrön (Buddhist, Tibetan Vajrayana, Karma Kagyü)
- Reverend Robert B. Dunbar (Christian, Episcopalian)
- Dr. Ibrahim Gamard (Muslim, Sunni, Mevlevi Sufi Order)
- Father Thomas Keating (Christian, Roman Catholic, Order of Cistercians of the Strict Observance)
- Roger La Borde (nonaligned)
- Tania Leontov (Buddhist, Tibetan Vajrayana)
- Reverend Donald H. Postema (Christian, Calvinist, Christian Reformed Church of North America)
- Rabbi Schlomo Schwartz (Jewish, Hasidic, HaBaD)
- Father George Timko (Christian, Eastern Orthodox)

Observer
- Elaine Postema

SNOWMASS IX
Tibet House, Crestone, Colorado (August 3–7, 1992)

Cancelled due to insufficient numbers. Nevertheless, Ibrahim Gamard drove to Colorado, unaware of the cancellation. He and his wife stayed at Roger La Borde's home and had discussions with him there.

SNOWMASS X
St. Benedict's Monastery, Snowmass, Colorado (May 31–June 4, 1993)
- Reverend Robert B. Dunbar (Christian, Episcopalian)
- Dr. Ibrahim Gamard (Muslim, Sunni, Mevlevi Sufi Order)
- Gesshin Prabhasa Dharma Roshi (Buddhist, Zen, Rinzai School)
- June Fog (Jain)

- Father Thomas Keating (Christian, Roman Catholic, Order of Cistercians of the Strict Observance)
- Roger La Borde (nonaligned)
- Tania Leontov (Buddhist, Tibetan Vajrayana)
- Reverend Donald H. Postema (Christian, Calvinist, Christian Reformed Church of North America)
- Rabbi Schlomo Schwartz (Jewish, Hasidic, HaBaD)

SNOWMASS XI

St. Benedict's Monastery, Snowmass, Colorado (May 1–5, 1994)

- James Barnett (Formerly Swami Buddhananda, nonaligned)
- Reverend Robert B. Dunbar (Christian, Episcopalian)
- Dr. Ibrahim Gamard (Muslim, Sunni, Mevlevi Sufi Order)
- June Fog (Jain)
- Father Thomas Keating (Christian, Roman Catholic, Order of Cistercians of the Strict Observance)
- Roger La Borde (nonaligned)
- Dr. Susan Schrager (Sister Sudha) (Hindu, Vedanta, Order of Ramakrishna Brahmavadin)
- Reverend Donald H. Postema (Christian, Calvinist, Christian Reformed Church of North America)
- Rabbi Schlomo Schwartz (Jewish, Hasidic, HaBaD)

SNOWMASS XII

St. Benedict's Monastery, Snowmass, Colorado (May 8–12, 1995)

- Swami Atmarupananda (Hindu, Vedanta, Ramakrishna Order)
- James Barnett (formerly Swami Buddhananda, nonaligned)
- Reverend Robert B. Dunbar (Christian, Episcopalian)
- Dr. Ibrahim Gamard (Muslim, Sunni, Mevlevi Sufi Order)
- Rabbi Henoch Dov (Howard) Hoffman (Jewish, Hasidic)
- Father Thomas Keating (Christian, Roman Catholic, Order of Cistercians of the Strict Observance)
- Roger La Borde (nonaligned)

- Tania Leontov (Buddhist, Tibetan Vajrayana)
- Reverend Donald H. Postema (Christian, Calvinist, Christian Reformed Church of North America)
- Father George Timko (Christian, Eastern Orthodox)

SNOWMASS XIII

St. Benedict's Monastery, Snowmass, Colorado (June 26–30, 1996)

- Swami Atmarupananda (Hindu, Vedanta, Ramakrishna Order)
- Reverend Robert B. Dunbar (Christian, Episcopalian)
- Dr. Ibrahim Gamard (Muslim, Sunni, Mevlevi Sufi Order)
- Father Thomas Keating (Christian, Roman Catholic, Order of Cistercians of the Strict Observance)
- Irfan Ahmad Khan (Muslim)
- Roger La Borde (nonaligned)
- Tania Leontov (Buddhist, Tibetan Vajrayana)
- Reverend Donald H. Postema (Christian, Calvinist, Christian Reformed Church of North America)
- Yvonne Rand (Buddhist)
- Rabbi Schlomo Schwartz (Jewish, Hasidic, HaBaD)
- Father George Timko (Christian, Eastern Orthodox)

SNOWMASS XIV

St. Benedict's Monastery, Snowmass, Colorado (May 21–25, 1997)

- Swami Atmarupananda (Hindu, Vedanta, Ramakrishna Order)
- James Barnett (formerly Swami Buddhananda, nonaligned)
- Reverend Robert B. Dunbar (Christian, Episcopalian)
- Dr. Ibrahim Gamard (Muslim, Sunni, Mevlevi Sufi Order)
- Gesshin Prabhasa Dharma Roshi (Buddhist, Zen, Rinzai School)
- Rabbi Henoch Dov (Howard) Hoffman (Jewish, Hasidic)
- Father Thomas Keating (Christian, Roman Catholic, Order of Cistercians of the Strict Observance)

- Tania Leontov (Buddhist, Tibetan Vajrayana)
- Reverend Donald H. Postema (Christian, Calvinist, Christian Reformed Church of North America)

SNOWMASS XV

St. Benedict's Monastery, Snowmass, Colorado (May 27–31, 1998)

- Swami Atmarupananda (Hindu, Vedanta, Ramakrishna Order)
- James Barnett (formerly Swami Buddhananda, nonaligned)
- Reverend Robert B. Dunbar (Christian, Episcopalian)
- Dr. Ibrahim Gamard ((Muslim, Sunni, Mevlevi Sufi Order)
- Rabbi Henoch Dov (Howard) Hoffman (Jewish, Hasidic)
- Father Thomas Keating (Christian, Roman Catholic, Order of Cistercians of the Strict Observance)
- Roger La Borde (nonaligned)
- Tania Leontov (Buddhist, Tibetan Vajrayana)
- Reverend Donald H. Postema (Christian, Calvinist, Christian Reformed Church of North America)

SNOWMASS XVI

St. Benedict's Monastery, Snowmass, Colorado (April 28–May 1, 1999)

- Swami Atmarupananda (Hindu, Vedanta, Ramakrishna Order)
- Dr. Edward W. Bastian (Buddhist, Tibetan Vajrayana, Geluga)
- Roland Cohen (Buddhist, Tibetan Vajrayana)
- Reverend Robert B. Dunbar (Christian, Episcopalian)
- Dr. Ibrahim Gamard (Muslim, Sunni, Mevlevi Sufi Order)
- Rabbi Henoch Dov (Howard) Hoffman (Jewish, Hasidic)
- Father Thomas Keating (Christian, Roman Catholic, Order of Cistercians of the Strict Observance)
- Roger La Borde (nonaligned)
- Reverend Donald H. Postema (Christian, Calvinist, Christian Reformed Church of North America)
- Father George Timko (Christian, Eastern Orthodox)

SNOWMASS XVII
Vivekananda Retreat, Stone Ridge, New York (May 24–28, 2000)

- Swami Atmarupananda (Hindu, Vedanta, Ramakrishna Order)
- Reverend Robert B. Dunbar (Christian, Episcopalian)
- Dr. Ibrahim Gamard (Muslim, Sunni, Mevlevi Sufi Order)
- Rabbi Henoch Dov (Howard) Hoffman (Jewish, Hasidic)
- Reverend Donald H. Postema (Christian, Calvinist, Christian Reformed Church of North America)

SNOWMASS XVIII
St. Benedict's Monastery, Snowmass, Colorado (March 24–28, 2004)

- Swami Atmarupananda (Hindu, Vedanta, Ramakrishna Order)
- Dr. Edward W. Bastian (Buddhist, Tibetan Vajrayana, Geluga)
- Reverend Robert B. Dunbar (Christian, Episcopalian)
- Dr. Ibrahim Gamard (Muslim, Sunni, Mevlevi Sufi Order)
- Rabbi Henoch Dov (Howard) Hoffman (Jewish, Hasidic)
- Father Thomas Keating (Christian, Roman Catholic, Order of Cistercians of the Strict Observance)
- Roger La Borde (Shaman)
- Tania Leontov (Buddhist, Tibetan Vajrayana)
- Reverend Donald H. Postema (Christian, Calvinist, Christian Reformed Church of North America)
- Srimata Sudha Puri (formerly Sister Sudha / Dr. Susan Schrager) (Hindu, Vedanta, Order of Ramakrishna Brahmavadin)

Observers
- Kathakali
- Elaine Postema
- Mary Purcell

THE SCHEDULE AND PROTOCOLS OF THE SNOWMASS CONFERENCE

BUSINESS MEETINGS AND OFFICERS

- Toward the end of each conference, a business meeting is held for members only. The purpose of the meeting is to make motions; to elect new officers; to discuss finances, changes to group process, the future of the group and guests; and to speculate about the next year's meeting (location and possible topics).
- The offices of the Snowmass Conference are: president, vice president/treasurer, and secretary.
- The president will lead the group discussion the next year and will issue formal invitations to the conference. The names of possible guests are sent to the president, who takes up the case of various candidates with the group members.
- The vice president/treasurer is responsible for dealing with the finances of the group.
- The secretary is in charge of communications between members. The secretary will contact each member around the turn of the year to confirm the retreat. At each conference there is an attempt to find a mutually agreeable time for the conference between major holy days.
- The officers also create schedules, discuss financing options and decide on the overall logistical plan of the next conference.
- The current secretary reads the minutes of the last meeting, keeps the minutes of the current meeting and distributes these to the group.

LOGISTICS, LOCATION, AND SUPPORT

- A spiritual center with room for dialogue and silent meditation is the optimal location for the conference. It is best if the center can even accommodate the participants as guests. If this is not possible, adequate housing must be arranged so that members can be as near to one another as possible.

- Either a member, or an agent of the group, must take the responsibility for making travel arrangements, coordinating different arrival and departure times and arranging for drivers. This person should also arrange for the appropriate support staff to prepare meals according to the different dietary requirements.

BASIC SCHEDULE

- Silent Meditation (30 min. to 1 hr.)
- Breakfast Together (45 min. to 1 hr.)
- Break (either omitted or 30 min. to 1 hr.)
- Dialogue Session (2 hr. to 2 hr. 15 min.)
- Lunch (45 min. to 1 hr.)
- Break (either omitted or 1 hr. to 2 hr. 15 min.)
- Silent Meditation (either omitted or 30 min. to 1 hr.)
- Dialogue Session (1 hr. 30 min. to 2 hr. 30 min.)
- Silent Meditation (either omitted or 30 min. to 1 hr.)
- Supper (45 min. to 1 hr.)
- Dialogue Session (1 hr. to 1 hr. 15 min.)

BIOGRAPHIES

2004 CONTRIBUTORS

Swami Atmarupananda (or Swami Ananda) hails from South Carolina, and joined the Ramakrishna Order in December of 1969, spending seven years in India engaged in monastic and scholastic training. He has served as minister for several communities, is a founding member of the Interreligious Council of San Diego, has lectured and published widely and was the founder and resident minister of the Vivekananda Retreat, Ridgely, New York.

Swami Atmarupananda has lectured, taught, led retreats and participated in multifaith dialogues throughout the United States and Mexico. Swamiji combines a contemplative and mystical approach with a sharp intellect and the ability to explain difficult concepts of Hinduism to a Western audience.

Dr. Edward W. Bastian earned a Ph.D. is in Buddhist studies and Western philosophy from the University of Wisconsin. He conducted research using Tibetan and Sanskrit languages for a number of years in India as a Fulbright Fellow and recipient of grants and fellowships from the Smithsonian and the American Institute of Indian Studies. In India, he lived in Tibetan monasteries and studied Indian philosophy and religion at Banares Hindu University. He has taught courses and moderated discussions on religion for the Smithsonian on Buddhism and world religions. He also has taught and lectured at a variety of educational venues and presented scholarly papers and films at academic conferences in the U.S., England, Japan and India.

Bastian was the executive producer for a series of six award-winning television programs on religion in India, Bhutan and Japan for the BBC, and produced a series of three films on Tibetan Buddhism with funding from the National Endowment for the Humanities, the U.S. Office of Education and the Smithsonian Institution. The production of these films drew heavily on the expertise of indigenous scholars and the films have been generally recognized for their sensitivity, depth and authenticity.

Bastian has directed several nonprofit organizations and has been a business executive, most recently as president of Aspen.com, an Internet company in Colorado. He also consults with spiritual institutions and media organizations and sits on various nonprofit and public interest boards. Presently, he is President of Spiritual Paths Foundation, which is producing seminars, books, television programs and a Web site on spirituality, based on a methodology he has developed in collaboration with authentic exemplars from the world's major spiritual traditions.

Reverend Robert B. Dunbar, an Episcopal priest, was born in Chester, South Carolina, in 1932. He has lived and exercised his ministry in Newark, New Jersey; Boston and Cambridge, Massachusetts; Beaufort, South Carolina; and places in between. He acknowledges the suffering to humanity and the world that the old rivalries and conflicts between the great religious traditions have caused (and sometimes cause without any competition). Can the old faiths be redeemed to make for peace and happiness instead of hatred and fear, mutual esteem instead of mere tolerance? His membership in the Snowmass Interreligious Conference is his gesture of hope that religion may prove to be healthy for the human race after all.

Dr. Ibrahim Gamard is an amateur Rumi scholar, born in the United States in 1947. A student of Sufism since 1971, Ibrahim was initiated into the Mevlevi Order in 1976 as a "whirler" (*semazen*). This is the tradition of Islamic mysticism, popularly known as the "Whirling Dervishes," that derives from the teachings and practices of Jalaluddin Rumi in the thirteenth century. Ibrahim has continued to participate in the famous Mevlevi "Whirling Prayer Ceremony" up to the present time. He is a disciple of a ninety-four-year-old Mevlevi *sheikh* in Istanbul, Turkey, who is under the authority of the present world leader of the Mevlevi order, the thirty-third Chelebi Efendi, and twenty-second-generation great-grandson of Hazrat-i Mevlana Jalaluddin Rumi. Ibrahim officially converted to Sunni Islam in 1984, and in 1999 fulfilled the requirement of every Muslim (who can afford it) to make the *Hajj* (pilgrimage) to Mecca.

Though professionally a licensed psychologist in California with a Ph.D. (1986) in psychology from the California Institute of Integral Studies, Ibrahim's passion is studying and translating the poetry of Rumi in his spare time. Around 1981, he began teaching himself classical Persian for the sole purpose of reading Rumi's poetry in the original language. And in 1985 he began collaborating with Dr. Ravan Farhadi, an Afghan professor of Persian literature at the University of California, Berkeley, in a translation of the nearly two thousand quatrains attributed to Rumi, together with commentary and Persian text, in what is presently an eight-hundred-page unpublished manuscript (entitled *The Quatrains of Rumi*).

In 1997, Ibrahim began posting articles on the Internet concerning Rumi translation issues, and over the next couple of years he was invited by a Rumi listserve group ("Sunlight" at yahoogroups.com, which offers daily translations and versions of Rumi's poetry) to add Persian transliterations to selections from R. A. Nicholson's (1926–1934) literal translation of the *Masnavi* (Rumi's masterpiece), and to post his own literal translations of selections from the *Masnavi* on "Sunlight" on a weekly basis. In 1999, he began work on his own Web site (dar-al-masnavi.org), which contains all the *Masnavi* selections he has translated over the years (with commentary and transliteration of the Persian).

Recently, Ibrahim wrote an introduction to *Hafiz: The Mystical Poets* (Skylight Paths, 2004) and published his own book of literal translations of Rumi, *Rumi and Islam* (Skylight Paths, 2004). This work contains translations and commentary on many of the beautiful things Rumi said about the Prophet Muhammad in his poetry and prose: stories about his virtues, quotations of his wise sayings and praises of his wonderful qualities.

Ibrahim has presented at two international Rumi conferences—"Rumi: Poet of Heart, Light of Mind," Columbia University, New York City (June 1997), and "Rumi 2000," California State University, San Bernardino (October 2000)—and once at the "Sufism Symposium," San Francisco (April 1999). Most recently, Ibrahim gave a talk entitled "Themes of Peace and Love in the *Masnavi* and Quatrains of Mawlana Rumi" at an international conference, "Conflict Resolution: A Dialogue Among Culture and Religions," at Union Theological Seminary, New York City (April 2002).

Rabbi Henoch Dov Hoffman received his B.A. *cum laude* in comparative religion from Dartmouth College in 1968, earned his M.A. from Antioch 1969, and pursued a Ph.D. in education at University of Colorado at Boulder, 1971–1978. Later, Rabbi Hoffman studied psychodrama with Dr. Carl Hollander at the Colorado Psychodrama Institute and was certified as a psychodrama therapist in 1980.

In 1972, he began his rabbinic studies, which he pursued under the guidance of two of the great Hasidic teachers of the twentieth century, Rabbi Shloime Twerski and Rabbi Shlomo Carlebach. He received his rabbinical ordination in 1992. Today, Rabbi Hoffman is a pastoral counselor, and a popular teacher of Torah and Hasidism in Denver, Colorado.

Father Thomas Keating was born in New York City in 1923 and entered the Order of Cistercians of the Strict Observance in Valley Falls, Rhode Island, in 1944. He was named Superior of St. Benedict's Monastery, Snowmass, Colorado, in 1958, and was elected Abbot of St. Joseph's Abbey, Spencer, Massachusetts, in 1961. He returned to Snowmass after retiring as abbot of Spencer in 1981. Father Keating is internationally renowned as a teacher of Christian contemplation, dedicating many years to the furtherance of contemplative work and the application of the contemplative perspective to ecumenical understanding and international peace.

Father Keating is one of the architects of the Centering Prayer movement and Contemplative Outreach, an organization designed to foster the Christian contemplative tradition through the practice of Centering Prayer. He was the chairman of the North American Board of East–West Dialogue, fostering exchange between monks and nuns of the world religions; a member of the board of directors of the Temple of Understanding since 1982 (chairman in 1984, which included the Sixth Summit Conference held in New York City), founding member of the Spirituality branch of Integral Institute and convener in 1984 of the Snowmass Interreligious Conference. He is the author of many books, including: *Open Mind, Open Heart*; *The Mystery of Christ*; *Invitation to Love*; *Intimacy with God*; *Crisis of Faith, Crisis of Love*; *Awakenings, Re-awakenings*; *Fruits and Gifts of the Spirit*; and *Manifesting God*.

Father Keating is one of the world's most widely recognized and revered teachers of the contemplative and mystical dimensions of Christian spirituality. He travels extensively throughout the world to Contemplative Outreach organizations, colleges and interreligious dialogues. He resides at St. Benedict's Monastery in Snowmass, Colorado, where a retreat facility focuses on his teachings of Centering Prayer. This spiritual practice emphasizes the ancient Christian traditions of mysticism, contemplation, meditation and prayer.

Roger La Borde was born in Port Arthur, Texas, in 1945. He graduated from the University of Houston with a degree in psychology, and worked from 1967 to 1979 for Humble Oil, Exxon Research, Pullman Kellogg, Fluor, and Tenneco Oil Company in Houston, Texas. In 1976, Roger went through a life-changing experience that eventually led him to abandon his career and move to an island near Seattle, Washington, in 1979. In 1982, Roger and his family were formally adopted by the Red Elk family on the Fort Peck Indian Reservation. The adoption made

Gerald Red Elk, a Yanktonai Sioux shaman, Roger's uncle, and a
teacher who continued to help Roger "open the door" to the
shaman's path.

Today, Roger is a healer recognized by Grandfather Gerald
Red Elk, Rolling Thunder, Don Eduardo Calderon Palomino,
and a number of other Native American medicine people. Roger
has been featured on the television shows, *Sightings*, *The Other
Side* and *That's Incredible*, as well as featured in an article in the
1994 issue of *The New Age Journal* for his successful work with
"no hope" coma cases. His healing work in all areas of illness has
taken him to Taiwan, France, Israel, Canada, Brazil and extensively throughout the United States. Roger and his family moved
to Colorado in 1982, where he currently resides. He is married
and has a son and two daughters. More information about Roger
and his work can be found at his Web site, shamansdoor.com.

Tania Leontov is the director of the Boulder County taskforce
Restoring the Soul: Faith and Community Partnerships, and the
director of the Buddhist Coalition for Bodhisattva Activity. She
was a director and meditation teacher at the Boulder Shambhala
Center for thirteen years. She also cofounded the Boulder-Lhasa
Sister City Project. Although engaged in nonprofit organizations
for more than thirty years, she was for a period of time an entre-
preneur of four successful businesses. Currently, she also teaches in
the graduate and undergraduate schools of Regis University in the
departments of nonprofit management, religion and philosophy.

Netanel Miles-Yepez was born in Battle Creek, Michigan, in 1972,
and is descended from a Sefardi family of crypto-Jews (*anusim*,
"forced" converts), tracing their ancestry from Mexico all the
way back to medieval Portugal and Spain. He studied history of
religions at Michigan State University and contemplative religion
at Naropa University, specializing in nondual philosophies and
comparative mysticism. Unsatisfied with academics alone,
Netanel moved to Boulder, Colorado, to become "reacquainted"
with his family's lost tradition of Judaism and to study Hasidism
under Rabbi Zalman Schachter-Shalomi's personal guidance.

Today, he is the cofounder of the Sufi-Hasidic Fellowship with Reb Zalman and an ordained *murshid* ("guide") of the Chishti-Maimuniyya Order of Dervishes, fusing the Sufi and Hasidic principles of spirituality espoused by Rabbi Avraham Maimuni in thirteenth-century Egypt.

Netanel is currently the executive director of the Reb Zalman Legacy Project, the editor of print and Web site publishing for the Spiritual Paths Foundation, and the editor of *The Way of Contemplation and Meditation* and *Wrapped in a Holy Flame: Teachings and Tales of the Hasidic Masters.* He lives with his wife, Jennifer, in Boulder, Colorado.

Reverend Donald H. Postema was born in 1934 in Chicago, Illinois, and is an ordained minister in the Christian Reformed Church of North America. He is a graduate of Calvin College and Calvin Theological Seminary, Grand Rapids, Michigan, and of the Vrije Universiteit van Amsterdam, the Netherlands. He has also studied at the Graduate Theological Union, Berkeley, California, and at Yale Divinity School, New Haven, Connecticut, with Fr. Henri J. M. Nouwen.

For thirty-four years, Reverend Postema served as a campus pastor at the University of Michigan, Ann Arbor. Since his retirement in 1997, Reverend Postema carries on a ministry of spiritual formation through retreats, conferences, writing, spiritual direction and teaching. He has served as a member of the adjunct faculty at Fuller Theological Seminary, Pasadena, California, at San Francisco Theological Seminary, and at Mars Hill Graduate School, Seattle, Washington. Reverend Postema has traveled widely both in the U.S. and abroad as a retreat leader and conference speaker. He is also the author of two books, *Catch Your Breath: God's Invitation to Sabbath Rest* and *Space for God: Study and Practice of Spirituality and Prayer,* in which he develops a "spirituality of gratitude."

Reverend Postema is a past president of the Snowmass Interreligious Conference and was twice their representative to the Parliament of the World's Religions. He has been deeply influenced by the music, meditation and attitudes of the ecumenical community of Taizé, France. From that community he learned that spirituality is basic for reconciliation among Christians, which also could provide ferment for peace and reconciliation among the world religions and in the human family. In exploring spirituality and art, Reverend Postema has been intrigued with Vincent van Gogh, whom he considers one of his spiritual guides. Travel, music, art, world religions, gardening, sports, writing and being with his wife, Elaine, and their four children and twelve grandchildren are among his other interests.

Srimata Sudha Puri was born in Los Angeles as Susan Schrager and grew up in Marin County in Northern California. She received her bachelor's degree in English, *magna cum laude*, at the University of Arizona in Tucson while she was a member of a religious teaching order. She went on to earn a master's degree in secondary education, with a specialization in reading disabilities, and a doctorate in educational psychology with supplementary specialization in school administration and law from the University of Southern California.

She has had a long and distinguished career in education, serving in teaching and administration in both the private and public schools, consulting, leading professional seminars, making frequent television appearances throughout the United States, conducting research, evaluating federal grant reading programs in public school systems, writing children's books and teaching in the graduate schools of education at both the University of Southern California and the University of California, Los Angeles. She has received many honors for her contribution to education.

At the age of fourteen, she was introduced to Eastern philosophy and has been a lifelong student of the great religions of the world. In 1980, she entered a spiritual community with a monastic tradition founded in India by the great Sankaracharya in the ninth century. Swami Paramananda was the founder of the Vedanta Center (1909) in Boston; Ananda Ashram (1923) and the two ashrams in Calcutta. He was the youngest monastic disciple of Swami Vivekananda who brought the philosophy of

Vedanta to the West in 1893. Sister Sudha's teacher was Reverend Mother Gayatri Devi, the first India woman to teach Vedanta in the West. Reverend Mother Gayatri Devi was the spiritual leader and minister of all the centers from the death of Swami Paramananda in 1940 until her passing in 1995. Trained and ordained by Reverend Mother Gayatri Devi, Reverend Mother Sudha was empowered to be her successor, the first American woman to have this role. In addition to her spiritual leadership, she oversees the retreat centers, the book publishing department, conducts public services and classes at the centers and gives spiritual instruction.

MEMBERS STILL WITH US . . . IN SPIRIT

Srimata Gayatri Devi (1906–1995) was born on October 12, 1906, in Dacca, East Bengal (now Bangladesh). Her father, a civil lawyer, was very prominent in civic affairs, strongly advocating education for women, human rights and freedom.

Reverend Mother Gayatri Devi represented Indian spirituality and taught Vedanta in many religious forums all over the world during her fifty-five years of leadership. In 1975, she addressed the Conference of World Religions at the United Nations, sharing the platform with Mother Teresa of Calcutta. She was a founding member of the Snowmass Religious Leaders Conference, an ecumenical group of spiritual leaders from a wide array of religious traditions working together to broaden and to deepen understanding among the religious traditions and their followers. In 1989, she was one of five master teachers of different world religions giving meditation and spiritual instruction at the Harmonia Mundi Contemplative Congress where His Holiness the Dalai Lama received the Nobel Peace Prize.

For decades, Mataji divided her time between Ananda Ashram in La Crescenta, California, and Vedanta Centre in Cohasset, Massachusetts, where she conducted Sunday services, meditation, and study classes, performed the worship services, gave spiritual instruction, cooked delicious Bengali offerings for the Shrine on special holy days, sang songs of Tagore and other Indian mystics and administered the work around the world. She was invited to speak before civic, religious and educational groups around the world.

She passed away in full spiritual consciousness on September 8, 1995, at the age of eighty-nine, having offered sixty-nine years of consecrated monastic service and fifty-five years as an inspiring and holy spiritual teacher, a *sat guru*.

Gesshin Myoko Prabhasa Dharma Roshi (1931–1999) was born in Frankfurt, Germany, on March 30, 1931, and moved to the United States in the 1950s. She entered Zen training in Los Angeles in 1967 under the Japanese Zen master Joshu Kyozan Denkyo-Shitsu Sasaki Roshi. A year later, she was ordained a nun. In 1972, she was recognized as a Zen priest and teacher (*osho*), and received the name Geshhin Myoko ("Moon Heart Brilliant Light"). She trained for more than a year at Tenryu-ji in Japan under the Zen master Seiko Hirata Roshi. She acted as director and vice abbot of both Mount Baldy and Cimarron Zen Center in Los Angeles. In 1983, she founded the International Zen Institute of America in Los Angeles, later establishing branches in Florida, the Netherlands, Germany, and Spain. She was given the "Dharma Mind Seal Transmission of a Great Master" by the Vietnamese Zen master Venerable Thich Man Giac in Los Angeles in April 1985, and received the name Thich Minh Phap (Sanskrit: *Prabhasa Dharma,* "Wondrous Light"), becoming the forty-fifth–generation heir in the lineage of Vietnamese Rinzai Zen. In 1996, she founded the International Zen Center Noorder Poort in the Netherlands. Her talk from the retreat "Being Buddha" is included in the book *Buddhism Through American Women's Eyes* (Snow Lion, 1995).

The beloved and respected Zen master Gesshin Myoko Prabhasa Dharma departed this manifest world on May 24, 1999, at her home in Marina del Rey, California. Through her many years of teaching, a strong following developed around Venerable Gesshin, known as the Moon Heart Sangha, which will continue her lineage. She will be remembered and missed by friends and disciples around the world. For further information: International Zen Institute of America and Europe, 1760 Pomona Avenue, no. 35, Costa Mesa, CA 92627, or www.zenin-stitute.org/en/home.html.

Grandfather Gerald Red Elk (1920–1985) of the Yanktonai Lakota Sioux, was born in Poplar, Montana, on January 20, 1920. Gerald was a "code talker" in the South Pacific during World War II, along with several others from the Fort Peck Indian Reservation. He was the historian and senior elder of the Rides a White Horse Clan, the curator and historian of the of the Fort Peck Reservation Museum, and an advisor to the Indian section of the Denver Museum of Natural History and the Smithsonian. Gerald Red Elk was widely known and respected in the Native American world as a *pejuta wicasa* ("medicine man"), shaman, and *wakan wicasa* ("holy man"). He passed away on October 21, 1985, in Poplar, Montana, at the local health clinic with his family by his side.

Douglas V. Steere (1901–1995) was professor emeritus of philosophy at Haverford College and for six years chairman of the Friends World Committee for Consultation. His devotional and scholarly writings included *On Beginning from Within*, *Doors into Life*, *On Listening to Another*, and *On Being Present Where You Are*. He traveled to many parts of the world on missions for the American Friends Service Committee and other Quaker organizations. He lectured extensively throughout the nation and in other countries. He was an observer-delegate of the Society of Friends at three sessions of Vatican Council II. During a journey with his wife, Dorothy, he organized and took part in "conversations in depth" between Christian and Buddhist scholars in Japan and Christian and Hindu scholars in India, under sponsorship of the Friends World Committee for Consultation. His books *Together in Solitude* and *Quaker Spirituality* continue his concern for the centrality of contemplation.

Father George Timko (1925–2000) was one of the senior priests of
the Diocese of New York and New Jersey. Fr. George was one of
the most remarkable of men. He was also an Orthodox pastor
without peer. He was a true original, unconventional, and a non-
conformist. He did not fit into any mold or any variation of what
a "typical" Orthodox priest might be, which led many to misun-
derstand and/or ignore his extraordinary talents. He knew the
Church Fathers better than most of us, yet he was clean-shaven
and shunned traditional monastic garb and prayer beads. He
fasted longer and more consistently than any other person I have
known, yet you could have a beer with him and discuss politics
or science as you would with any average fellow. He prayed and
meditated intensely.

Fr. George grew up around hard-working people in the min-
ing region of western Pennsylvania. He never hid the fact that he
began his life as a coal miner, where he learned to respect and
appreciate honest manual labor. He was, first of all, a scriptural
man. He loved the Bible, studied it thoroughly, and always
turned to it. To this normative foundation he brought a phenomenal knowledge and veneration for the Church Fathers (he read
and reread the volumes of the spiritual masterpiece called the
Philokalia, as well as many other writings), whom he regarded as
accomplished guides and the best exponents of Orthodox
Christianity. Because there are so few living experienced elders in
our time, he constantly reminded us that the writings of the
Fathers are indispensable in our spiritual formation. Spirituality
also determined his approach to liturgy. On the surface, Fr.
George seemed to have a novel approach to the liturgy. Actually,
his liturgical style was inspired and inspiring. For him, religious
ritual always corresponded with spiritual growth in love and
peace.

He appreciated ecumenical dialogue, which he saw as a
means for sharing truth and deepening his own faith. He participated in interfaith discussions and meetings on a variety of levels, where he was a recognized authority on Eastern Christian
spiritual life. Fr. George saw Orthodoxy as having become free of
the burdens of social and cultural attachments. In times past,

these were intrinsic to the Church's life, but widespread secularism and scientific revolutions have changed that. As a political and cultural force, the Orthodox Church has minimal if any effect in our society, yet the profound truths of Orthodox spirituality, which are also the heart of our theological tradition, are fresh, valid and relevant. With zeal and pastoral care, Fr. George enlightened his spiritual flock and colleagues into an appreciation of these values and made us calmer and wiser in the process.

Fr. George Timko passed away on November 18, 2000, at the age of seventy-five. Fr. George suffered a debilitating aneurysm in the fall of 1999, which forced him to retire as pastor of St. George Church in Buffalo, New York, where he had served almost thirty years. We cherish the memory of his honest sense of Christian freedom, hard earned by years of difficult trials and transitions. A guileless man, he resisted preconceptions and prejudices of all kinds. He would question and challenge things that many of us were afraid or unable to. He always spoke the truth with conviction. In the course of life, only a few like Fr. George Timko come along. For those who were privileged to know him he was impressive in many ways: a blessed gadfly, a dynamic preacher, a gifted speaker, an insightful observer of life and a courageous witness at ecclesial gatherings. He was also a profound Orthodox thinker, a working-class hero and a prophetic voice. (Adapted from "In Memoriam: Fr. George Timko" by Fr. Alexander Garklavs)